Pursuit
of the
Impossible Dream

By Dee Brown CEO

DEDICATION

To my mother, whose love was a steady flame that neither poverty nor illness could extinguish. You gave everything so that we could have more, and in doing so, you gave me the greatest inheritance of all: the belief that I was worth the sacrifice.

Your journey—from hardship to healing, from struggle to service—proved to me long before I ever set foot in a boardroom that ordinary people can do extraordinary things when they refuse to quit.

Though you are no longer here to witness the chapters still unfolding, your spirit walks with me in every room I enter and every door I open for someone else.

To my grandfather, who, with only a third-grade education, taught me what it means to show up, to provide, and never to abandon your children. You were the father figure who shaped my understanding of commitment and manhood. My son, Brandon Edward, carries your name and legacy forward.

To William Neil Griffin, my mentor and the most significant male figure in my life, aside from my grandfather. Though we lost touch and I never got that final conversation, your belief in me and that first investment loan started everything. My son, Jujuan William, carries your name and legacy forward.

And to everyone who dared to dream despite the odds, who refused to accept "impossible" as the final answer, who chose to "get it out the mud" and build something meaningful—

This book is for you.

The sky isn't the limit. It's just the beginning…

Table of Contents

DEDICATION iii

PROLOGUE...vi

CHAPTER 1 – THE FOUNDATION 1

CHAPTER 2 – DREAM BIG 8

CHAPTER 3 – EDUCATION IS YOUR FOUNDATION 16

CHAPTER 4 – BREAKING BARRIERS...........................28

CHAPTER 5 – THE FALL AND THE RISE 39

CHAPTER 6 – THE P3 PHILOSOPHY 50

CHAPTER 7 – RESILIENCE THROUGH ADVERSITY.....................60

CHAPTER 8 – DIVERSIFY YOUR VISION 70

CHAPTER 9 – GIVE BACK TO RISE HIGHER...................82

CHAPTER 10 – BRAND YOURSELF 94

CHAPTER 11 – LEADERSHIP AND INFLUENCE 100

CHAPTER 12 – THE SKY'S THE LIMIT...............................106

CHAPTER 13 – YOUR BLUEPRINT FOR SUCCESS.....................113

PROLOGUE

I'm standing on a street that bears my name.

Dee Brown Lane. In Clarksdale, Mississippi. The same street where I used to play football and kickball as a kid, dreaming dreams I didn't yet have the language to articulate.

It's June 2025, and my hometown has just honored me with this recognition. But as I stand here, surrounded by community members and local officials, I'm not thinking about the honor. I'm thinking about the person who should be here but isn't.

My mother passed away two years ago, in August 2023, after a long battle with breast cancer. In her final days, she showed me what true strength looks like—facing death with remarkable courage and clarity, refusing to be sedated even as her body failed her. I was there. I held her hand. I witnessed the transition from life to death.

That moment changed everything for me.

My mother's death profoundly shaped the way I view life. Watching her face cancer with courage and choose not to endure painful treatments that might have extended her life at the cost of its quality made me think of Shakespeare's line, "A coward dies a thousand times." In her, I witnessed not a coward, but a heroine who died only once.

Her strength reminded me how often people let fear and imagined failure steal their opportunities. It also made me realize that time is finite, and we must live fully, seize each opportunity, and take nothing for granted.

All the success I'd built, all the barriers I'd broken, all the wealth I'd accumulated—none of it could save her. And in that profound helplessness, I understood something I'd been too busy achieving to fully grasp. Success isn't about what you accumulate. It's about what you contribute. It's about the lives you touch while you're here.

Standing on this street named in my honor, I realize that my mother walked these same streets countless times—exhausted from working multiple jobs, sacrificing everything so her children could have what she never had. She never got to see this street sign. She never got to stand here and see her son honored by the community she served.

But she saw something more important: She saw me become the man she raised me to be.

This book is about pursuing impossible dreams. But it's also about understanding why those dreams matter. It's about recognizing that every achievement is built on someone else's sacrifice. It's about honoring the people who believed in you before you believed in yourself.

My mother showed me what's possible when you refuse to let circumstances defeat you. She showed that dignity and values matter more than advantages. She proved that hard work and integrity can transform not just your own life, but the lives of everyone around you.

Now it's my turn to show you what she showed me.

This isn't just my story. It's a blueprint for anyone who's been told their dreams are too big, their background is too limited, or their circumstances are too difficult. It's for anyone ready to prove that 'impossible' is just another word for 'untried'.

The street may bear my name, but the legacy belongs to everyone who dared to dream despite the odds.

Let's begin.

CHAPTER 1 –
THE FOUNDATION

Welcome to a journey that I hope will ignite something powerful within you. I'm Dee Brown, and I stand before you today as someone who has walked through fire, climbed mountains, and refused to accept limitations placed on me by others or by circumstance. I want to share my story with you, not from some pedestal of achievement, but as someone who's walked a path filled with struggles, doubts, and hard-won victories.

I'm the Founder and CEO of The P3 Group Inc., the nation's leading African American-owned public-private partnership real estate development firm, but more importantly, I'm someone just like you, someone who's faced obstacles, questioned myself, and had to find the courage to keep going when everything seemed impossible.

When I look back at my career spanning over three decades in real estate development, sales, and management, I see more than just buildings and contracts. I see a testament to what's possible when you combine unwavering dedication with an unshakeable belief in your vision. I see communities transformed, lives changed, and barriers broken that many said could never be moved. I see faces, the families who found homes, the young people who got opportunities, the communities that came back to life. I see my mother's sacrifices reflected in every project. I see the struggles that shaped me into who I am today. And I see proof that dreams really can come true, even when you start with nothing but hope and determination.

Here's what I want you to understand from the very beginning: this has never been just about business for me. Every project I've undertaken, every deal I've closed, every building I've developed has been driven by a deeper purpose. I've been trying to prove something—to myself, to my community, and to everyone who ever doubted that someone like me could achieve this. More than that, I've been trying to create something that would outlast me: something that would make my mother proud and open doors for others. Each step has been a deliberate move toward fulfilling larger ideals and executing projects that transcend mere buildings.

Success isn't built on luck. It's built on the cornerstones of careful preparation and an unwavering commitment to quality. I learned early on that excellence isn't negotiable—watching my mother work multiple jobs and still find time to make sure we had what we needed. It's built on preparation, yes, but also on heart: caring deeply about the work you do and the people you serve.

Excellence became non-negotiable for me—not because I read it in a business book, but because I saw what happened when people cut corners in my community: families living in substandard housing, neighborhoods neglected, promises broken. I decided I would never be that person. I would never deliver less than my best. Over the years, The P3 Group has distinguished itself not just by material success, but also by its goal of creating lasting places that benefit the communities in which they are located.

Let me tell you something that fires me up every single day: I've made a name for myself in the world of entrepreneurship as a visionary with a flair for creativity and as a business leader. But what really fires me up is knowing that the work we do changes lives. When I see a family move into quality affordable housing, when I see a student get to attend college because of our student housing developments, when I see a community come back to life, it makes all the long hours and hard work worth it.

The P3 Group is a remarkable example of how commercial opportunities and strategic vision can work together to set new industry benchmarks. We didn't just enter the real estate development industry; we revolutionized it by skillfully combining the resources of the public and private sectors. I'm deeply proud of The P3 Group—not because of its size or success, but because of what it stands for. We brought together public resources and private innovation to build what communities truly need. We didn't just enter an industry; we changed how it works, proving that you can be profitable while being purposeful, and that you can build wealth while building communities.

My journey's story is one of innumerable talks, complex transaction structures, and the skill of transforming prospects into reality. It's about having a sharp eye for detail, about using that eye to navigate the complexity of real estate, overcoming obstacles, and coming out on top when designing environments that are pleasing to the sight and the senses.

My journey has been filled with countless conversations, complex negotiations, and the daily work of turning vision into reality. But it's also been filled with doubt, with setbacks, with moments when I wasn't sure I could pull it off. I've learned to pay attention to details not because I'm naturally meticulous, but because I've seen what happens when details are overlooked, projects fail, people get hurt, and communities suffer. So, I learned to care about every aspect, to fight for quality, to never settle for "good enough" when people's lives and livelihoods are at stake.

But my approach involves more than simply building structures. It's about shaping communities. It's about creating thriving environments that enhance people's lives and strengthen the socioeconomic fabric. But here's what I realized early on: buildings are just buildings unless they serve people. What matters is the lives that unfold within those walls, the communities that grow around them, and the opportunities they create. I'm not just building structures—I'm trying to build hope, to create spaces where families can thrive, where children can grow up safely, where communities can come together and support each other. This philosophy has helped The P3 Group and me establish a reputation as leaders in public-private partnership real estate development—a shining example of inclusion and success.

Here's something I'm incredibly proud of: I approach the world of charity with the firm conviction that one's ability to positively influence society, rather than just achieving financial gain, is what truly defines success. It means everything to me: I believe neither your bank account nor your awards measures genuine success. It's measured by the difference you make in people's lives. My mother taught me that. She had almost nothing materially, but she gave everything she had to her children and her community. That's the wealth that matters. That's the success I'm chasing. This idea is explored in action by the Brown Foundation Community Development Corporation, which is committed to improving communities, advancing education, and nourishing the aspirations of future generations.

I didn't write this book to boast about my achievements. I wrote it because I believe that within each of you reading these words right now, there's untapped potential waiting to explode into greatness. I wrote it because someone needs to hear that being the first doesn't mean you have to be the last. I wrote it because your background, your zip code, and your circumstances, none of these things have the final say in your destiny. I didn't write this book to impress you with my accomplishments. Honestly, I wrote it because I wish someone had written it for me when I was starting, when I was scared, when I was doubting myself, when I felt like the odds were impossibly stacked against me. I wrote it because I know there's someone out there right now who feels the way I used to feel, like their dreams are too big, like their circumstances are too limiting, like success is for other people, not for them.

I'm writing to tell you that's not true. Your background doesn't have to be your destiny. Your zip code doesn't determine your worth. Your circumstances are your starting point, not your ending point.

Throughout these thirteen chapters, I'm going to share with you the principles, strategies, and mindset shifts that took me from humble beginnings to becoming the first African American owner of an 18-hole golf course in Arkansas, to building the nation's leading African American-owned public-private partnership real estate development firm, to creating a media empire, a fashion line, a tequila brand, and even owning a 100-foot luxury yacht.

But more importantly, I'm going to show you how YOU can apply these same principles to your own life, regardless of your industry or the dreams you're chasing.

The sky isn't the limit—it's just the beginning.

After 32 years of building businesses and breaking barriers, here are the five things I wish someone had told me before I started—lessons that would have saved me pain, accelerated my success, and made the journey smoother:

LESSON 1: YOU MUST BE TOUGH, BUT CARING

To be a successful CEO, you must be tough and thick-skinned, but you must also care about your employees and their families, the clients you serve, and your organization's reputation. Sometimes it's difficult to make tough decisions that affect the people you care about, but as a CEO, you must be able to do so.

This balance is one of the hardest things to master. You can't be so soft that you avoid necessary decisions, but you can't be so hard that you lose your humanity. The best leaders I know have figured out how to hold both to make tough calls while genuinely caring about the people affected by those calls.

Here's a specific example of this from my experience—one of the most difficult periods of my leadership.

As CEO of The P3 Group, I've had moments when I've felt acutely alone. One of the most difficult was having to terminate three employees—people I was very close to—in close succession. Because I genuinely cared about each of them, it was a painful decision, and one I made largely in isolation.

They were all in leadership positions, and each had strong relationships not only with me but also with other leaders within our organization. I didn't want to place the burden of making such a tough decision on anyone else's shoulders, so I carried it alone.

I spent more than a few sleepless nights under the weight of those choices—not simply because I ended their employment, but because I worried about them as friends and people. I worried about the impact a sudden loss of income and stability could have on their lives and their families.

In my heart, I know I didn't have a choice. The organization's health required these decisions. But the part of me that saw them not just as colleagues, but as friends, carried it heavily.

These are the kinds of decisions I take no pleasure in making, especially because they can permanently alter, and sometimes irreparably damage, the personal side of those relationships. That's the cost of leadership that nobody talks about. It's what "tough but caring" feels like in practice.

LESSON 2: PROCRASTINATION IS THE POISON THAT KILLS DREAMS

As a CEO, you must be able to make quick and decisive decisions. Opportunity only knocks once, and your inaction can be costly to your organization and the bottom line. Delaying the termination of a toxic employee or starting a time-sensitive project late and missing the deadline can all have catastrophic effects on your organization.

I've seen more dreams die from hesitation than from failure. People wait for the perfect moment, the perfect plan, the perfect conditions—and while they're waiting, the opportunity passes them by. Speed matters. Decisiveness matters. Taking action even when you don't have perfect information matters.

LESSON 3: GETTING YOUR DAY STARTED BEFORE EVERYONE ELSE GIVES YOU A WINNING EDGE

We all have 24 hours in a day, but how we use those hours determines our level of success. I found early on that if I get up around 3:30 AM, I can accomplish tasks that are nearly impossible when the demands of a hectic day weigh on me. Early mornings allow me to do research, write contributing articles, create goals, and establish objectives for my company. It's also a great time to exercise and meditate.

Those quiet hours before the world wakes up? That's when I do my best thinking, my most strategic planning, my deepest work. No phone calls. No meetings. No interruptions. Just me, my vision, and the work that moves everything forward.

LESSON 4: YOU MUST BE PRINCIPLED

I had to learn that to be a successful CEO, you must establish principles and live by them. There must be guard rails that always keep you in bounds—these are the principles to which you subscribe. By establishing principles and living by them, you can protect your character and reputation.

Your principles guide you when no one is watching. They're what keep you on track when temptation arises. They're what allow you to sleep at night knowing you did the right thing, even when the right thing was hard or costly. Without principles, success becomes hollow. With them, success becomes meaningful.

LESSON 5: NEVER HIRE SOMEONE YOU CAN'T FIRE

As a CEO, you may be tempted to hire people you know or have a relationship with. This is fine, but you must have the mental toughness to manage, and if necessary, discipline or terminate anyone you hire.

This lesson cost me dearly before I learned it. I've hired friends, family members, and people I felt obligated to. And when they didn't perform, I struggled to hold them accountable because of the relationship. That's not fair to them, to your other employees, or to your organization. If you can't imagine having the difficult conversation or making the hard call, don't make the hire.

These five lessons represent wisdom earned through mistakes, through struggles, through learning the hard way. I'm sharing them with you so you can learn from my experience instead of repeating my mistakes.

CHAPTER 2 –
DREAM BIG

Every great achievement begins with what others call impossible. This chapter is about the pursuit of the impossible dream, the audacious vision that defies logic and challenges convention.

Let me ask you something: When was the last time you allowed yourself to dream without boundaries? When was the last time you envisioned something so massive, so audacious, that it scared you a little? When was the last time you let yourself really dream? Not the safe, practical dreams that everyone approves of, but the wild, audacious dreams that make your heart race? The dreams that scare you and excite you at the same time?

I'm talking about the dreams that make people look at you sideways. The kind that makes your family members pull you aside and ask if you're "being realistic." The kind that keeps you up at night, not with worry, but with excitement so intense you can barely contain it. You're lying there in the dark, seeing it all play out in your mind, feeling it, believing it's possible even when logic says it's not.

That's where greatness lives. Right there in that uncomfortable space between what is and what could be.

When I first envisioned The P3 Group becoming the nation's leading African American-owned public-private partnership real estate development firm, people thought I was dreaming. People thought I'd lost touch with reality. Public-private partnerships? In real estate development? At that scale? As a minority-owned business? The odds were stacked so high against me that most people couldn't even see the top.

Your dreams should be so big that they require you to grow into them. If you can accomplish your dream with your current skills, knowledge, and resources, then friend, you're not dreaming big enough.

Let me tell you about the first time I learned this lesson—long before I entered the business world.

My first experience with dreaming big and growing into that dream goes back to middle school. As I will discuss in more detail later, my mindset changed after sixth grade. I adopted the belief that I could accomplish anything I set my mind to. But believing it and proving it are two different things.

From fifth through eighth grade, I played trumpet in the band. I had never played an organized sport; my only experience came from playing sandlot football, kickball, and baseball. The summer before my ninth-grade year, I decided I wanted to run track. I'd spent the first part of the summer sitting around, listening to different runners talk about their times and speed in different races. There was a long-distance runner from my neighborhood whose athleticism I admired, Gregory Pace. Greg was fast, disciplined, and successful. I wanted to emulate him.

So I decided: I was going to run the mile and be part of the mile relay team.

Here's where it gets interesting: I went to the track coach, Curtis Kemp, and told him, with complete confidence, that I could run a mile in 4 minutes and 58 seconds.

The truth? I had never run a timed mile in my entire life. Not once. I pulled that time straight from conversations I'd overheard from Greg and other runners. I did not know if I could actually do it.

But I also knew something important: I had time to train. I had the entire summer to become the track star I'd just claimed to be. I'd made the declaration. Now I had to grow into it.

That's exactly what I did.

All summer long, I ran all over Clarksdale relentlessly. I ran in the morning heat. I ran in the evening. I ran when I was tired. I ran when I didn't feel like it. I was training for a goal I'd announced before I'd earned the right to claim it.

When the season started, something remarkable happened: I went undefeated in the mile. I won every single race. My mile relay team was also undefeated, and we advanced to the state championship.

At the state meet, I finished second in the mile. My relay team took first place.

It was an unbelievable season. But more than the wins, more than the medals, more than the recognition—it taught me something fundamental about how dreams work.

I had declared a capability I didn't yet have. Then I worked relentlessly to grow into that declaration. I didn't wait until I was ready. I didn't wait until I'd proven I could do it. I claimed it first, then became it.

That pattern, dream it, declare it, then grow into it, became the blueprint for everything I've achieved since. From that track in Clarksdale to building The P3 Group, the principle has remained the same: dream so big that you have to become someone new to achieve it.

But here's what I discovered: your dreams should stretch you. They should require you to become someone you're not yet. If you can achieve your dream with who you are right now, with what you know right now, with what you have right now, then honestly, you're playing it too safe. Dream something that scares you. Dream something that requires you to grow, to learn, to become more than you currently are.

I didn't just want to be in real estate. I wanted to transform how real estate development works. I wanted to create a model that brought together public resources and private innovation to build communities that served the people living in them. I wanted to prove that you could do well financially while doing good for society. I didn't just want a job in real estate.

I wanted to show that doing well and doing good weren't opposites; they could be partners. That dream seemed impossible to most people. But to me? It was inevitable because I had already seen it completed in my mind.

Let me share something powerful with you: Everything that exists in our physical world was once just a thought in someone's mind. The phone you're holding, the building you're sitting in, the car you drive—all of it started as an idea that someone refused to let go of.

Your dreams work the same way. They're not just fantasies. They're blueprints for your future reality.

But dreaming big isn't just about the size of your vision. It's about the courage to pursue it even when the path isn't clear. When I became the owner of a golf course, I didn't have a roadmap. There was no manual titled "How to Break Barriers in Golf Course Ownership." I had to create the path by walking it.

And you know what? That's exactly what you're going to have to do with your dreams, too.

Here's the truth that nobody tells you: The bigger your dream, the more resistance you'll face not just from others, but from yourself. Your own mind will try to talk you out of it. It'll remind you of every failure, every limitation, and every reason you're not qualified.

That voice? That's not wisdom. That's fear dressed up as common sense. Here's something I need to be honest with you about: the bigger your dream, the louder the doubts become. And the worst doubts? They don't come from other people. They come from inside your own head. That voice that says, "Who do you think you are?" That voice that reminds you of every time you've failed before. That voice that lists all the reasons you're not qualified, not ready, not enough.

I still hear that voice sometimes. Even now, after everything I've achieved, that voice still shows up when I'm about to try something new.

But I've learned something: that voice isn't trying to guide you. It's trying to protect you from disappointment, from failure, from looking foolish. It's fear wearing a mask of wisdom.

I've learned to recognize that voice, thank it for trying to protect me, and then move forward anyway. Because on the other side of that fear is everything you've ever wanted. So now when I hear it, I acknowledge it. I say, "Thank you for trying to keep me safe," and then I do the thing anyway because I've learned that everything I've ever wanted, every breakthrough, every achievement, every moment of real joy has been on the other side of that fear.

When I expanded beyond real estate into media production, launching Self Made Entertainment and Self Made TV, people questioned it. "Stick to what you know," they said. When I started my podcast, "The Sky's the Limit: Beyond the Deal," in collaboration with Forbes Books, some wondered whether I was spreading myself too thin. When I launched my luxury clothing line and tequila brand, the skeptics multiplied.

But here's what they didn't understand: I wasn't diversifying randomly. I was following a vision that was bigger than any single industry. I was building a brand, a movement, a legacy that would inspire people across multiple platforms and touchpoints.

Your dream should be big enough to encompass multiple expressions of your purpose. Don't let anyone box you into being "just" one thing.

Now, let me give you some practical wisdom about dreaming big: Write it down. Seriously. Get specific. Don't just say, "I want to be successful." Define what success looks like for you in vivid detail. How much revenue? How many people are you impacting—and in what way? What does your day look like? What does your legacy look like?

I've kept journals throughout my entire career, documenting not just what I've accomplished but what I'm working toward. There's something powerful about putting pen to paper. It takes your dream from the ethereal realm of "someday" and plants it firmly in the soil of "I'm making this happen."

Second, surround yourself with people who dream as big as you do—or bigger. I'm a life member of Kappa Alpha Psi Fraternity Incorporated, a life member of the NAACP, the Producers Guild of America, and many other organizations. These aren't just networking opportunities. They're communities of excellence where big dreams are normalized rather than ridiculed.

Show me your five closest friends, and I'll show you your future. If everyone around you is comfortable with mediocrity, you'll have to fight twice as hard to pursue excellence. But if visionaries, innovators, and action-takers surround you? Your big dreams become the baseline, not the ceiling.

Third, act immediately. Don't wait until you have it all figured out. Don't wait until the conditions are perfect. Don't wait until you feel ready. You will never feel completely ready for something you've never done before.

I didn't wait until I had every detail of public-private partnerships figured out before I started The P3 Group. I learned by doing. I made mistakes, adjusted, and kept moving forward. Every single day, I took at least one action that moved me closer to my vision.

That's the secret: Big dreams require daily action. Not monthly. Not when you feel inspired. Daily.

This is what's crucial: Your big dream isn't just about you. The most powerful dreams are the ones that lift others as you rise. When I founded the Brown Foundation Community Development Corporation, it wasn't separate from my business success—it was integral to it.

I realized that my dream of building a real estate empire would be hollow if it didn't strengthen the communities I worked in. True success isn't measured just by what you accumulate, but by what you contribute.

So, as you're dreaming big, ask yourself: Who else benefits when I achieve this? How does my success create opportunities for others? What legacy am I building beyond my bank account?

When your dream is connected to a purpose larger than yourself, you'll find reserves of energy and determination you didn't know you had. You'll push through obstacles that would stop someone who's only motivated by personal gain.

Let me tell you about a moment that crystallized this for me. In 2013, I became the first minority Department of Defense contractor to hold a prime federal contract with the U.S. Navy Nuclear Power Training Unit at Goose Creek, South Carolina. It wasn't just a business milestone. It was proof that barriers could be broken, that "firsts" were possible, that the impossible was just the untried.

But more than that, it opened doors for other minority contractors who came after me. My big dream created a pathway for others to dream big, too.

That's the ripple effect of an audacious vision. When you achieve something that people say couldn't be done, you don't just change your own life. You expand the realm of possibilities for everyone watching.

So, here's my challenge to you: What's the dream you've been too afraid to speak out loud? What's the vision that seems so impossible that you've kept it locked away in the back of your mind?

Bring it out. Dust it off. Look at it in the full light of day.

Now make it bigger.

I'm serious. Whatever you just thought of, double it. If you're thinking about starting a business, don't just think about one location—envision a national presence. If you're thinking about writing a book, don't just think about self-publishing—envision it on the New York Times bestseller list. If you're thinking about making a difference in your community, don't just think about helping a few people—envision transforming the entire community.

Why? Because you're going to face obstacles regardless of the size of your dream. You might as well face them while pursuing something extraordinary rather than something ordinary.

I've won over 150 awards across more than 14 countries as an executive producer, director, and talk show host. I've received recognition from the U.S. Small Business Administration, Forbes magazine, Inc. Magazine, the Congressional Black Caucus, the Thurgood Marshall Legacy Award from the U.S. Minority Contractors Association, and even the U.S. President's Lifetime Achievement Award from President Biden. But none of these accolades came from playing it safe. They came from dreaming bigger than anyone expected and then having the audacity to make those dreams a reality.

Your dreams are valid. Your vision is possible. Your goals are achievable. But only if you're willing to think bigger than you ever have before.

The world doesn't need more people playing small. It needs more people who will dream big, act boldly, and inspire others to do the same.

So, dream big. Dream so big that it scares you. Dream so big that you have to grow into a new version of yourself to achieve it. Because that's exactly what you're capable of.

Dreaming big isn't just optimism; it's the foundation for pursuing the impossible dream. Every barrier I've broken, every first I've achieved, started as a dream that seemed impossible to everyone else.

Now let's talk about how to build the foundation that will support those massive dreams…

CHAPTER 3 –
EDUCATION IS YOUR FOUNDATION

The pursuit of the impossible dream requires a foundation strong enough to support it. That foundation is education, not just degrees, but a lifelong commitment to learning that equips you to achieve what others say can't be done.

Let me tell you something that changed the trajectory of my entire life: Education is not just about degrees on a wall. It's about building an unshakeable foundation strong enough to support the weight of your dreams. Education became my way out. Not just out of poverty, but out of the limitations that poverty tries to impose on your thinking. It became my ticket to rooms I never thought I'd enter, to conversations I never thought I'd be part of, to opportunities I never thought were meant for someone like me.

To better understand my educational journey, it helps to know where I come from.

I grew up in the rural Mississippi Delta, in the small town of Clarksdale, and was raised by a single mother. We lived in a two-bedroom house with my grandparents, my uncle, my brother, and my mother. My mother lived in poverty during her childhood and early career. I saw the struggle. I felt it. I watched my mom literally work 16-hour shifts.

My grandfather, who only had a third-grade education, was the only father figure I had for most of my early years. He taught me what it meant to be a man and to be there for your family. He was firm; he disciplined me as a child, but as I grew older, he became someone I could confide in. He was a constant presence in my life until his death in March 1997. The absence of my biological father lit a fire inside of me, but my grandfather showed me what I should aspire to be—a man who shows up, who provides, who never abandons his children. That example shaped everything about how I approach my commitments today. One of my sons has my grandfather's name as his middle name.

As I mentioned previously, my mindset first changed when I was in the sixth grade. This change began after I took a reading comprehension test and performed poorly on it. The embarrassment I felt at being taken out of the class with my peers and sent to a reading lab changed my life.

To compound an already devastating experience, the summer after sixth grade, my grandmother died in August, and my grandfather never walked again. In the aftermath, my mother moved my brother and me to Memphis in search of better financial opportunities. I was devastated—not only by my grandmother's death and my grandfather's declining health, but also by being uprooted from the only home I had ever known.

We remained in Memphis for seventh and eighth grade, then returned to Clarksdale the summer before ninth grade as my grandfather's health declined, ultimately resulting in the first of his two leg amputations.

Somehow, enduring this series of events strengthened my resilience at an early age. Through these experiences, I became mentally tough and committed to achievement and success. After sixth grade, I became an honor student, graduating from high school as class president with the highest GPA among student athletes.

Think about that transformation: From struggling with reading comprehension and enduring multiple life-changing events to class president with the highest GPA; from a household where my grandfather only had a third-grade education to becoming an honor student; from feeling embarrassed in sixth grade to leading my class by senior year.

That's the power of education. That's what happens when you decide that your circumstances don't define your destiny. That's what's possible when you channel embarrassment into determination, when you transform struggle into fuel for achievement.

But my mother's educational journey was happening alongside mine, and it would transform both of our lives in ways I couldn't have imagined.

My mother became a licensed practical nurse after graduating from high school and had to work long, grueling hours to make ends meet. I watched her leave for work exhausted and come home even more exhausted, sacrificing her own comfort so we could have what we needed.

But she didn't stop there. She returned to school and became a Registered Nurse. She went back and completed her associate's degree, becoming a Registered Nurse. And she still didn't stop. She completed her bachelor's degree and then her master's degree.

Her education transformed our lives economically. As an RN with advanced degrees, she earned significantly more money. We weren't wealthy, and she still worked long hours, but we were no longer in poverty. Going back and completing her education literally changed our lives.

The timing mattered: Her transformation happened at the start of my high school years, when stability and opportunity make a lasting difference in a young person's life. For the first time, I had a weekly allowance. For the first time, my mother could buy both my brother and me our own cars—changes that completely reshaped what I believed was possible for our lives.

That new sense of possibility sparked something else in me: an early instinct for structuring deals and solving problems creatively.

During my senior year of high school, I saw a 1990 Geo Tracker on a dealership showroom floor and became determined to get it. I walked into the dealership, spoke with the salesperson who knew my family, and asked to call my mother's banker. Although I'd never met him personally, I knew he handled my mother's financing and had supported my previous car purchase. I also knew that the bank was a big supporter of my high school football team, and I was a popular player, having won the bank's player-of-the-week award many times.

I told the banker exactly what I needed: structure the financing so I could trade in my current car, pay off the existing debt, and ensure the monthly payment matched what my mother was already paying. He ran the numbers and agreed to those terms.

Minutes later, the dealership owner handed me the keys—even though I was 18 years old, had no job, hadn't filled out any paperwork, and had no proof of insurance.

I was excited until I got into the vehicle, because only then did I realize the Geo Tracker was a five-speed manual transmission—which I'd never driven in my life. I called a friend, Sean Cummings, who talked me through driving a manual transmission over the phone, and somehow, I drove that SUV home.

When my mother arrived home shortly after, she was stunned to see me in a different vehicle. She wanted to know whose car I was in, and I explained it was her graduation present to me. I told her that the paperwork was ready at the bank and reassured her that the monthly payment hadn't changed.

Still in disbelief, she went to the bank and confirmed everything. Years later, she admitted she signed the paperwork partly because she couldn't believe I had pulled off what looked like an impossible deal.

That moment became my first real experience with creative transaction structuring, solving a problem by focusing on the terms that mattered most and making the numbers work, even in an unlikely situation. It showed me that with the right approach, you can structure opportunities that seem impossible to others.

My mother's journey from LPN to a master's degree showed me it was possible. My journey from that reading lab to class president proved I could do it. Together, these experiences taught me that education isn't just about escaping poverty; it's about transforming your entire sense of what's possible for your life.

But let me be honest with you about the start of my real estate career—it didn't begin with much pomp and circumstance. I left college with one semester left in my senior year, much to my mother's dismay, to begin a career in real estate. I was moving from the rural Mississippi Delta into a field where African Americans were virtually invisible—real estate. My mother thought I should finish my degree, and I had only one semester left. I ultimately finished my bachelor's and master's degrees, but not before taking the big plunge into the real estate industry.

Looking back, I understand my mother's concern. She wanted me to have that degree, that credential, that proof of achievement. She knew how hard it was for African Americans to succeed without every advantage. And she was right to push me.

Sometimes you must take a leap before you feel completely ready. Sometimes the opportunity in front of you is too compelling to wait. The key is that you come back and finish what you started. I eventually returned to school and finished those degrees because I understood that education wasn't just about the piece of paper. It was about the knowledge, the credibility, and the foundation for everything I wanted to build. It was also my way of setting benchmarks for my children and grandchildren.

My mother's insistence on education, even when I was impatient to get started, taught me something crucial: You can pursue your dreams AND invest in your education. They're not mutually exclusive. In fact, they reinforce each other.

She showed me, through her own life, that it's never too late to invest in your education and that the sacrifice is worth it. Education is one of the few things that can genuinely change your family's economic path.

I hold a bachelor's degree from the University of Memphis and an MBA from Bethel University. I've earned many professional certifications throughout my career. But here's what I want you to understand: These credentials weren't just pieces of paper to hang in my office. They were tools that equipped me to compete at the highest levels, to speak the language of business, and to command respect in rooms where I was often the only person who looked like me.

But let me be real with you about what those degrees really meant: They were my armor. They were proof that I belonged in rooms where people who looked like me weren't usually welcome. They were the credentials that made it harder for people to dismiss me, to underestimate me, to assume I didn't know what I was talking about. Were they enough to overcome all bias? No. But they gave me a fighting chance. They gave me the knowledge and confidence to compete at the highest levels.

Education gave me something that nobody could ever take away: Knowledge. Competence. Confidence.

When I walked into negotiations for multi-million-dollar construction projects, I wasn't just bringing my ambition. I was bringing expertise backed by formal education, real-world experience, and continuous learning. That combination is unstoppable.

But let me be clear about something: Education doesn't stop when you walk across a graduation stage. That's just the beginning. The most successful people I know are perpetual students. They're always learning, always growing, always expanding their knowledge base.

I have been a contributing writer for Forbes.com, Entrepreneur.com, Metro Magazine, and Peoria Magazine. Why? Because writing forces you to clarify your thinking. It forces you to stay current with industry trends. It forces you to articulate your insights in ways that add value to others. That's education in action.

I serve on the Documentary and Nonfiction Committee for the Producers Guild of America. I'm a member of the National Academy of Television, Arts & Sciences, the International Documentary Association, and the Entrepreneur Leadership Network. These aren't just titles to add to my bio. They're learning communities where I'm constantly exposed to new ideas, best practices, and innovative thinking.

That's the kind of education that keeps you relevant, competitive, and ahead of the curve.

Here's what I've learned about education over my 32-year career: The more you know, the more opportunities you can recognize and capitalize on. When I first started in real estate development, I could have stayed in my lane. But I invested in learning about public-private partnerships—a complex field that most people avoid because of its intricacy.

That education opened an entirely new market for me. It allowed me to create The P3 Group and build it into the nation's leading African American-owned firm in that space. That didn't happen by accident. It happened because I was willing to do the hard work of learning something new, something difficult, something that most of my competitors weren't willing to tackle.

Education is your competitive advantage. It's what separates you from the pack.

Let me show you exactly how education and industry knowledge translate directly into business success with a concrete example.

When the city of Pine Bluff entered into a development agreement with The P3 Group to design, build, and finance the demolition of its abandoned convention center hotel and its replacement with a new 125-room Courtyard by Marriott, most people believed it couldn't be done. Not in a small market like Pine Bluff, Arkansas. After all, this was a $25 million project in a community that had struggled economically for years.

What gave us the edge? Understanding, in advance, exactly what would make the deal financeable and legally executable. That understanding came directly from years of education—formal degrees, professional certifications, and continuous learning about finance, law, and public-private partnerships.

First, we assembled a top-tier legal and finance team with a proven track record of execution. But I also knew there was a narrow path to making this transaction work, and my education had taught me exactly what that path looked like.

The project had to start with a feasibility study that clearly supported demand and viability. Without that, neither the lender nor the public partner could responsibly move forward. This wasn't just a formality—it was the foundation on which everything else would be built. My MBA training taught me to read and interpret feasibility studies, challenge assumptions, and ensure the numbers were solid.

Next came financing. We evaluated the realistic options: an unrated bond transaction, a traditional bank loan, or, because Pine Bluff qualified by population, a USDA Guaranteed Loan. Based on my financial experience and education, I advised the team that USDA was the only viable option.

The reason is simple, but you must understand the mechanics: The USDA guarantee dramatically changes lender risk. USDA guarantees 80% of the loan amount. In practical terms, if a default occurs, the federal government covers 80% of the outstanding balance, leaving the lender with only 20% exposure.

That risk reduction is often the difference between a "no" and a "yes," especially in smaller communities where traditional lenders see too much risk. Knowing this—understanding the specific programs available, the qualification requirements, the application process—that's the knowledge that comes from education and experience working together.

But here's where it got even more complex: We had to structure the deal correctly under Arkansas law. A municipality cannot hold an ownership interest in a hotel—it can only own a convention center in Arkansas. That legal constraint could have stopped the project entirely.

Most developers would have walked away, but my education had taught me to look for creative solutions within legal frameworks. Working alongside The P3 Group, our legal team created a Public Facilities Board—the only quasi-governmental entity in Arkansas with the authority to hold an ownership interest in a hotel.

It was a detailed, heavily scrutinized process, especially because it was the first municipal hotel structure of its kind in the state. Every document had to be perfect. Every legal argument had to be airtight. Every financial projection had to be defensible.

That combination of financial knowledge, legal structuring, and disciplined execution is exactly how we turned what most people thought was impossible into a deliverable project. In February 2025, we broke ground on this project that many believed couldn't be done.

This is what I mean when I say education is your competitive advantage. Without my continuous learning, I wouldn't have understood the financial structuring required. Without my education, I wouldn't have known about USDA guarantees. Without my legal education and partnerships with expert attorneys, we couldn't have created the Public Facilities Board.

Education didn't just help me get this deal—education made this deal possible. That's the difference between having credentials on your wall and having knowledge you can deploy to solve complex problems and create opportunities.

Now, I know what some of you might think: "Dee, I can't afford to go back to school." Or "I don't have time for formal education." I hear you. But education comes in many forms, and in today's world, there's absolutely no excuse for not learning.

You have access to more information than any generation in human history. Online courses, podcasts, YouTube tutorials, industry publications, mentorship programs—the resources are endless. The question isn't whether you have access to education. The question is whether you're disciplined enough to pursue it.

I didn't just stop at my MBA. I pursued professional certifications that were directly relevant to my industry. I read voraciously. I attended conferences. I sought business associates who knew more than I did. I asked questions. I took notes. I implemented what I had learned.

That's the difference between people who succeed and people who stay stuck: Successful people are committed to continuous improvement through continuous learning.

Keep this practical advice with you: every single day, I set aside time to learn something new. It might be reading an industry publication, listening to a podcast, watching a documentary, or having a conversation with someone who has expertise I don't have. This isn't optional for me. It's as essential as breathing.

Why? Because the world is changing faster than ever before. The skills that got you here won't necessarily get you there. The knowledge that was cutting-edge five years ago might be obsolete today. If you're not learning, you're falling behind.

As I mentioned previously, I had the honor of being the first minority Department of Defense contractor to hold a prime federal contract with the U.S. Navy Nuclear Power Training Unit in Goose Creek, South Carolina. Do you think I could have achieved that without a deep knowledge of federal contracting, compliance requirements, and technical specifications? Absolutely not. I had to educate myself on every aspect of that process and do so at a level that exceeded my competitors' standards.

Education gave me that edge.

Here's another truth about education: It builds credibility. When I speak at conferences about public-private partnerships, people listen because I've done the work to become an expert. When I write articles for Forbes and Entrepreneur, editors publish them because I've built a knowledge base worth sharing. When I advise organizations on P3s, they value my input because I've invested years in mastering this field.

You can't fake expertise. You can't shortcut your way to credibility. You must put in the work.

But here's the beautiful thing about education: It compounds. Every book you read, every course you take, every skill you develop—it all builds on itself. Knowledge connects to knowledge. Skills reinforce skills. Over time, you become a powerhouse of expertise that nobody can compete with.

Let me ask you something: What are you learning right now? Not what did you learn in school ten years ago. Not what you plan to learn someday. What are you actively learning right now?

If you can't answer that question, you've got work to do.

Identify the gaps in your knowledge. What skills do you need to reach the next level in your career? What expertise would make you invaluable in your industry? What knowledge would give you a competitive advantage?

Then, create a learning plan. It doesn't have to be complicated. Start with one book per month. One online course per quarter. One conference per year. One mentor relationship. Just start somewhere and be consistent.

I also want to talk about the importance of diverse education. Don't just learn about your specific field. Learn about business, finance, marketing, leadership, communication, and technology. The most successful entrepreneurs are Renaissance people—they have broad knowledge across multiple disciplines.

That's why I didn't just focus on real estate. I educated myself about media production, which led to Self Made Entertainment and Self TV. I learned about fashion and lifestyle branding, which led to my luxury clothing line. I studied the spirits industry, which led to my tequila brand. I learned about maritime operations, which led to my yacht charter company.

Each of these ventures required me to become a student again, to humble myself and learn from experts, to invest time and energy into mastering new domains.

And you know what? That willingness to be a perpetual student has made my life infinitely more interesting, more profitable, and more impactful.

There is something else that's crucial: Education isn't just about what you know. It's about how you think. Formal education teaches you critical thinking, problem-solving, analytical skills, and the ability to synthesize complex information. These are transferable skills that serve you in every area of life.

When analyzing a potential real estate development project, I use the same critical thinking skills I developed in my MBA program. When I'm producing a television show, I apply the problem-solving methodologies I learned in my undergraduate studies. When I'm negotiating a contract, I'm leveraging analytical frameworks I've studied throughout my career.

Education shapes your mind, and your mind shapes your reality.

I also want to address something important: Education is not about being the smartest person in the room. It's about being the most prepared. My educational journey was itself a pursuit of an impossible dream. As I worked toward my bachelor's degree and MBA, I wasn't just collecting credentials—I was building a knowledge base that would allow me to break barriers and achieve what seemed impossible in real estate development.

It's about having done the homework so that when opportunity knocks, you're ready to answer.

I've been in countless meetings where I wasn't the most naturally gifted person present. But I was often the most prepared because I had done the research, studied the background, and educated myself on every relevant detail. That preparation has won me more deals than raw talent ever could.

So, here's my challenge to you: Commit to being a lifelong learner. Make education a non-negotiable part of your daily routine. Invest in yourself by reading books, taking courses, earning certifications, and gaining experience that expand your knowledge and capabilities.

Your education is the foundation upon which everything else is built. The stronger the foundation, the higher you can build.

Never stop learning. Never stop growing. Never stop investing in your own development.

Because the moment you stop learning is the moment you stop leading.

Education transforms impossible dreams into achievable goals. It's what gave me the tools to pursue opportunities that others couldn't even see. Invest in your education, and you invest in your ability to pursue your own impossible dream.

Now let's talk about what happens when you take that education and use it to break through barriers that others say are impossible...

CHAPTER 4 –
BREAKING BARRIERS

The pursuit of the impossible dream means confronting barriers that others accept as permanent. It means being the first when everyone says it can't be done. This chapter is about how breaking barriers isn't just about personal achievement; it's about proving that impossible dreams are simply dreams that haven't been pursued yet.

There's something exhilarating about being the first. There's also something terrifying about it.

When I purchased a golf course, I wasn't just buying a piece of real estate; I was making history. I was shattering a barrier that had stood for generations. I proved that what seemed impossible was untried.

Let's discuss how that deal came together, because it shows how opportunity often arrives when you least expect it.

The decision to buy the golf course happened almost out of the blue. The P3 Group owned about 85 acres directly south of the golf course, where we were developing Brownstone Estates Subdivision. My chief operating officer,

Grandon Gray, knew about this land, and one day he came to me with news: the golf course owner was interested in selling.

The timing was remarkable. I had just returned from Martin Downs Golf Club and Resort in Palm City, Florida, where I'd hosted a tequila tasting event. Martin Downs is also African American-owned, and during my visit, I spoke with one of the owners about the business. They shared something crucial: golf courses typically come with additional real estate development opportunities.

So, when Grandon brought this deal to me, I was already primed to see the possibilities.

I reviewed the opportunity and immediately saw something most people would have missed. This wasn't just about owning a golf course. I saw a unique opportunity to tie the Brownstone Estates homeowner's association to the golf course membership—a cost-effective way to provide premium amenities to our new community. The golf course was equipped with meeting space, a pro shop, a restaurant, and a swimming pool. I envisioned improving all these amenities to serve both the club and the new residential community we were building.

But I saw even more. I saw rezoning opportunities that would open the door to additional developments. As I write this book, we're building a gas station and convenience store on the property in partnership with Chevron. We're planning an RV park and waterpark on 6.7 acres at the golf course.

All these possibilities raced through my mind as I evaluated the deal. And forty-five days later, I owned what is now known as Brownstone Country Club & Resort.

That's how strategic vision works. It's not just about the deal in front of you. It's about seeing three, four, five moves ahead. It's about understanding how one acquisition can unlock multiple opportunities. It's about creating value that compounds over time.

But this is what nobody tells you about being the first: You're walking a path that doesn't exist yet. There's no blueprint. No mentor's done exactly what you're trying to do. There's no safety net of precedent to catch you if you fall.

You must create the path by walking it.

And that's exactly what I've done throughout my career—repeatedly.

But let's discuss my first business deal —the one that taught me I could create opportunities where none existed. This was early in my journey, before I even had formal training in real estate. My uncle owned about 600 acres of land, and he saw something in me—a spark, a hunger to build something meaningful. He made me an offer that would change my life: I could use his land to raise money for real estate school, but there was a catch—I couldn't sell the land itself. I had to figure out another way.

So, I did my research. I learned about timber sales, assessing the value of standing timber, and connecting with buyers. Then I went out and sold the timber on those 600 acres. I was successful. I raised the money I needed and used it to pay for real estate school. That timber sale wasn't just a transaction—it was my entry point into this entire industry.

It taught me that when you don't have traditional resources, you must be creative. You must see value where others don't. You must structure opportunities from what you have, not wait for what you don't have. My uncle believed in me enough to give me that chance, and I made the most of it.

That timber sale and the education it funded taught me something powerful: When you don't have traditional resources, get creative. Find ways to create value for everyone involved. Structure deals that make sense even when you don't have everything you need upfront.

That creative deal-making became one of my main strengths. It's what later allowed me to structure complex public-private partnerships. It's what enabled me to close deals that others couldn't figure out.

And it all started with that first lumber transaction, when I had more vision than capital, more determination than resources.

I took that first deal, and I made it work. I delivered on my commitments. I served the community. And I proved to myself—and to others—that I could do this.

That success led to the next opportunity, which led to the next, which led to the next.

That timber sale funded my real estate education. And my real estate school instructor, Paul Turner? He was the owner of Century 21 Action Associates in Germantown, Tennessee.

After I completed real estate school, I walked into his office for an interview, full of hope and determination, ready to prove myself as a sales associate. But I didn't do well in the interview. He made it clear—he didn't think I would be successful in real estate.

I could have let that rejection define me. I could have walked away and found something else. But he did something that changed my life: Despite his doubts, he still gave me a chance to join his firm and kick off my career in real estate.

Four months later, I became one of the firm's top salespeople.

Let that sink in. Four months. From "I don't think you'll be successful" to top producer. My instructor, who had taught me the fundamentals, didn't believe I could apply them successfully. But I proved him wrong through sheer hunger, a strong work ethic, and my refusal to accept his assessment as my reality.

But here's where the story gets even better: Four years later, I started my firm. And then I purchased Century 21 Action Associates—the very firm where I'd started, where my instructor and boss had doubted me. And Paul? He came to work for me.

Talk about the ultimate pursuit of the impossible dream. Talk about coming full circle. Talk about proving that other people's assessment of your potential means nothing compared to your own belief in yourself.

But there was someone who believed in me from the very beginning— someone who became one of the most significant influences in my life.

Early in my real estate career at Century 21, I met an attorney named William Neil Griffin. Everyone called him Will. He was a real estate attorney and developer, and he owned three banks. Will was someone I looked up to immensely, and I can honestly say he was one of the few people who was a true mentor to me.

Will really believed in me. He saw something in me that others didn't see, and he wanted to see me succeed. My very first investment loan came through his bank. Think about what that meant—a young African American real estate agent with more dreams than capital, and here was this successful businessman willing to back me with his own institutions. That wasn't just a business transaction. That was belief in action.

I deeply admired him as a businessman, and I always aspired to be like him. He showed me what success with integrity looked like. He showed how you could build wealth while maintaining your values. He proved you could be successful and still care about helping others rise.

My biggest regret is being unable to sit down and talk with him before he passed in December 2024. We lost touch over the years—you know how life gets busy, how time slips away, how you keep meaning to reach out but don't. When I finally reached out to reconnect, I learned he had dementia and likely wouldn't know who I was. That news hurt deeply.

When I learned of his death, I was devastated. Not just because I lost someone important to me, but because I never had that final conversation. I never got to tell him how much he meant to me, how much his belief in me shaped my entire career, how much I appreciated that first loan that started everything.

Even after we lost touch, Will's influence never left me. I credit him with much of my success. The way he conducted business, the way he treated people, the way he built multiple successful ventures—all of that became a model I studied and tried to emulate.

Will was perhaps the most significant male figure in my life, aside from my grandfather. And to honor his memory and his impact on my life, I gave one of my sons the middle name William. Every time I say my son's full name, I'm reminded of the man who believed in me when I was just starting out, who gave me opportunities when others saw only risk, who showed me what was possible through his own example.

That's the power of mentorship. That's the impact one person can have on another's life. That's why I'm so committed now to being that person for others, to be the Will Griffin in someone else's story.

That experience taught me something fundamental: When someone gives you a chance—even if they don't fully believe in you—take it and run with it. Prove them wrong. Exceed their expectations. Then keep going until you've achieved things they never imagined possible.

When I was awarded the Department of Defense contract at the U.S. Navy Nuclear Power Training Unit, I entered a space where people who looked like me were simply absent. The barriers weren't just professional; they were historical, systemic, and deeply entrenched.

Let me tell you what that project involved, because the complexity was unlike anything I'd ever faced.

I had to train my crane operators and riggers certified to operate a 500,000-pound Manitowoc crane—on a floating barge. Think about that: a barge on water, with a crane that weighs half a million pounds. The margin for error was zero.

Once we had successfully trained our employees at the shipyard in Goose Creek, tugboats transported the barge and crane into the nuclear facility. We were there to assist U.S. Navy riggers in changing 60,000-pound sea anchors on nuclear submarines.

Put this in perspective: I had never seen a nuclear submarine before this project, let alone a 60,000-pound sea anchor. This was by far the most complex, high-stakes project I had ever undertaken. The technical requirements, the security protocols, the precision needed, everything about it was operating at a level many contractors have never experienced.

And when we completed the project, the U.S. Navy gave us a performance rating of "very good"—a metric showing low risk and high-quality work. That rating meant everything. It meant we hadn't just met their standards—we'd exceeded them. It meant we'd proven ourselves in one of the most demanding environments possible.

It's what breaking barriers looks like in practice. It's not just about getting the opportunity. It's about delivering at such a high level you prove you belonged there all along.

Remember, barriers are only permanent if you accept them as such.

Every barrier is just a question: Are you willing to do what it takes to break through? Are you willing to work harder, learn more, persist longer, and believe more strongly than everyone who came before you and stopped at this same wall?

I was willing. And that made all the difference.

You must understand the psychology of breaking barriers. When you're attempting something that's never been done before—especially as a minority in spaces that haven't traditionally welcomed you—you face a unique form of pressure. You're not just representing yourself. You're representing everyone who looks like you, everyone who comes after you, everyone who's watching to see if it's possible.

That pressure can crush you or fuel you. I let it fuel me.

Every time I walked into a boardroom as the only African American person, I knew I had to be twice as prepared, twice as knowledgeable, and twice as professional—not because it's fair—it isn't, but because that's reality. I felt it. The eyes are on me. The assumptions. The unspoken questions about whether I really belonged there. It made me angry sometimes. It still does. But I had a choice: I could be angry and give up, or I could be angry and use that as fuel to prove every doubter wrong. I chose the latter.

I outworked everyone. I outstudied everyone. I out-prepared everyone. And slowly, steadily, I earned respect that couldn't be denied. So, I worked harder than anyone else. I studied longer. I prepared more thoroughly. I showed up earlier and stayed later. And slowly, painfully slowly sometimes, I earned respect. Not because people suddenly saw past their biases, but because my results were undeniable. When you consistently deliver excellence, people must acknowledge it, even if they don't want to.

Breaking barriers has taught me that excellence is the ultimate equalizer. When you're undeniably excellent at what you do, barriers crumble. Not because people suddenly become enlightened, but because they can't ignore the results.

The P3 Group didn't become the nation's leading African American-owned public-private partnership real estate development firm because of affirmative action or diversity initiatives. We became who we are by delivering results that exceeded expectations, time after time after time.

We completed projects on time and under budget. We navigated complex regulatory environments with expertise. We brought innovation to an industry that desperately needed it. We created value for our partners and our communities.

That track record spoke louder than any barrier could silence. But I want to be honest with you about something: Breaking barriers is exhausting. Sometimes I wanted to quit. Times when the obstacles seemed insurmountable. Times when I questioned whether it was worth the fight. Breaking barriers is emotionally, physically, and mentally draining. There were nights when I lay awake wondering if I was crazy to keep trying. Mornings when I didn't want to get out of bed and face another day of fighting uphill battles. Moments when I seriously considered just walking away from it all and finding an easier path.

In those moments, I had to remind myself why I was doing this. I wasn't just building a business. I was opening doors for the next generation. I was proving that limitations are lies. I was creating possibilities where none existed before.

That purpose kept me going when everything else told me to stop. In those dark moments, I had to dig deep and remember why this mattered. I'd think about my mother, working those multiple jobs, never complaining. I'd think about the young people in my community who needed to see that someone who looked like them could achieve this. I'd think about the doors that would open for others if I could just break through this one barrier.

One major barrier I had to break was access to capital. As a minority entrepreneur pursuing large-scale real estate development, I often faced skepticism from lenders. I responded by building credibility step by step: strengthening relationships one conversation at a time, proving my ability through smaller projects, assembling a strong team, and structuring deals to minimize lender risk. Most importantly, I consistently over-delivered—finishing projects on time or early, on budget or under, and with quality that exceeded expectations—until my track record spoke for itself.

Slowly, my reputation spoke for itself. Slowly, doors opened. Not because the system became fair, but because I became undeniable within that unfair system.

That's the reality of breaking barriers: Sometimes you must work within an imperfect system while simultaneously working to change it.

I also learned that breaking barriers requires allies. As a member of a fraternity and numerous professional organizations, I found communities that provided support, mentorship, and advocacy—each of which has contributed to my success.

You can't break barriers alone. You need people who believe in you, who open doors for you, who vouch for you when you're not in the room.

But here's the key: you must earn that support through your actions, character, and results.

I want to talk about something that's often overlooked when we discuss breaking barriers: The responsibility that comes with being the first. When you break through a barrier, you're not just creating opportunities for yourself. You're creating a pathway for others to follow.

That means you must succeed. Not just for yourself, but for everyone who's watching, everyone who's hoping, everyone who's dreaming that they might be next.

I take that responsibility seriously. That's why I founded the Brown Foundation Community Development Corporation. That's why I mentor young entrepreneurs. That's why I speak at conferences and write articles sharing what I've learned. That's why I'm writing this book.

Because being the first means nothing if you're also the last.

My goal has never been to be the only African American in these spaces. My goal has been to be the first of many. To prove it's possible. To create a template that others can follow and improve upon.

And you know what? It's working. I see more minority entrepreneurs in real estate development now than when I started. I see more diversity in public-private partnerships. I see doors opening that were previously locked.

That's the legacy of breaking barriers: You don't just change your own life. You change the landscape for everyone who comes after you.

Now, let me give you some practical advice about breaking barriers in your own life and career:

First, identify the specific barriers you're facing. Get clear about what's standing in the way of your goals. Is it a lack of access? Lack of knowledge? Lack of capital? Lack of network? You can't break through a barrier you haven't clearly identified.

Second, study those who've broken similar barriers. While you might be the first in your specific context, someone somewhere has overcome similar obstacles. Learn from their strategies. Adapt their approaches to your situation.

Third, build undeniable competence. This is non-negotiable. Be so good at what you do that people can't ignore you, can't dismiss you, can't deny you.

Fourth, document your journey. When you break through a barrier, share your story. Write about it. Speak about it. Teach others how you did it. Your breakthrough becomes a blueprint for others.

Fifth, bring others with you. As you rise, reach back. Mentor. Advocate. Create opportunities. The barriers you break should create pathways, not just personal success.

That's the real reward of breaking barriers: Expanding the realm of possibility for others.

I need you to understand that whatever barrier you're facing right now, it's not permanent. It's not insurmountable. It's not the end of your story.

It's just the next challenge to overcome.

And when you break through it—and you will break through it—you'll look back and realize that the barrier wasn't there to stop you. It was there to test you, to strengthen you, to prepare you for the even greater opportunities that lie ahead.

So don't run from barriers. Run toward them. Attack them with everything you've got. Break them down with excellence, persistence, and unwavering belief in yourself.

Because on the other side of every barrier is a breakthrough waiting to happen.

Every barrier I've broken was once someone's impossible dream. The golf course ownership, the Navy contract, building the nation's leading African American-owned P3 firm—each was impossible until it wasn't. That's the power of pursuing the impossible dream: You don't just achieve it for yourself, you prove it's possible for everyone who comes after.

Now, let's talk about my fall from grace—and how I fought my way back to the top against all odds...

CHAPTER 5 –
THE FALL AND THE RISE

Let me share the part of my story I've avoided talking about for years. The part that almost destroyed me. The part that taught me more about resilience, injustice, and redemption than anything else in my life.

It is the story of my greatest fall and my greatest comeback.

BUILDING THE EMPIRE

Remember when I told you I purchased Century 21 Action Associates, the very firm where I'd started, where my instructor initially doubted me? That was just the beginning.

My business partner and I renamed it **American Realty USA**, making it our second location. We had a vision: to build the largest minority-owned real estate firm in Tennessee.

Paul Turner, the original owner who had doubted me during that first interview, came to work for us as a corporate trainer and broker. Think about that full-circle moment: the man who didn't think I'd succeed was now training salespeople under my leadership. And we didn't just talk about being the largest, we made it happen.

Within a short period, American Realty USA grew to over 200 salespeople across three locations in Memphis. We weren't just big; we were dominant. We specialized in buying and selling HUD foreclosures, and we controlled 80% of that market from 1996 to 2000. Eighty percent. Let that sink in.

We were the go-to firm. We had the systems, the people, the expertise, and the market presence. I was in my late twenties, running the largest minority-owned real estate company in the state, making more money than I'd ever imagined possible.

I thought I had it all figured out. I thought I was untouchable.

I was wrong.

THE DEAL THAT CHANGED EVERYTHING

Around 1997, we were approached about purchasing a large portfolio of duplexes throughout Memphis. It wasn't unusual—we were doing deals like this regularly. But this one was different.

The deal was structured by bankers and lawyers I respected—people with sterling reputations and decades of industry experience. The structure they created required the seller to sell the property to a middle person, who would then sell it to my entity. It was a two-step transaction.

Now, I know what you might think: "That sounds suspicious." But here's the context: There were many real estate professionals throughout Memphis competing for and purchasing properties under this same structure. This wasn't some back-alley deal.

And I didn't just take their word for it. Multiple attorneys assured me that the transactions were legal. My brokers went out and got independent legal advice confirming the same thing. We did our due diligence. We followed the structure that the lenders and attorneys had approved.

Over a two-year period from 1997 to 1998, I acquired a substantial number of these properties. Business was booming. American Realty USA was thriving. Everything seemed to go exactly according to plan.

It was November 1999. I had just been named Entrepreneur of the Year for the state of Tennessee by the Small Business Administration, and almost simultaneously, Ebony Magazine named me to its Top 40 Under 40 list. Without question, it was the most exhilarating moment of my early career. But the celebration was short-lived.

Then the scrutiny began.

WHEN THE WALLS STARTED CLOSING IN

By late November 1999, the local newspaper had started investigating these transactions. Questions were being raised. And suddenly, the lender who had orchestrated this entire transactional structure, the very people who had created this model and assured us it was legitimate, called me to a meeting.

But I'd heard rumblings. I'd heard they were trying to insinuate that we had duped them into these transactions. That we had somehow manipulated them. So, I did something that would later prove crucial: I put a recorder in the inside pocket of my suit and went to that meeting.

What happened in that meeting was stunning.

The lender took full responsibility for the transactions and their structure. They assured me that I had done nothing wrong. They explained they were under pressure to sell the loans, but, because of negative publicity, could not do so, and their warehouse lines had to be paid off.

Then they made an extraordinary request: They asked me to take out a $5 million loan to pay off their warehouse lines. And they offered to co-sign the loans with me.

Think about that. The people who created this structure, who were now claiming there were problems with it, wanted me to bail them out with a $5 million loan they would co-sign.

I rejected that request. But I had the entire conversation recorded without their knowledge.

I thought that the recording would protect me. I thought the truth would set me free.

I was naïve.

THE INDICTMENT

Months after I rejected their request, the lender filed a civil lawsuit against me and others who had taken part in these transactions, alleging fraud, RICO violations, and other claims. I wasn't worried. I had the recording. I had evidence that they had orchestrated everything, that they had taken full responsibility, that they had even asked me to bail them out.

Shortly after I revealed through my legal counsel at that time, AC Wharton, that I had these recordings, something changed. We began receiving federal criminal subpoenas related to the transactions.

Even then, I was comfortable. I had done nothing wrong. I had the audio recording of the lender's confession. I had documentation. I had independent legal opinions confirming that the transactions were legitimate.

I met with federal investigators under a proffer agreement. They laid out their case, and I addressed every single point:

Point 1: Fraudulent Leases

They claimed there were fraudulent leases in the files. I submitted that I never created a false lease and that, if one existed, they should conduct a handwriting analysis to determine who created it and what their motive was.

I also explained to the investigators that there would have been no need to create fraudulent leases because my debt-to-income ratio would not have required it; therefore, whoever did it would have had no valid reason.

They later determined I didn't create any leases. But then they changed the narrative—claiming I directed someone else to do it. Someone who had their own financial incentives. There was no evidence to support this claim. None. But the narrative had shifted.

Point 2: Inflated Appraisals

They stated that the appraisals were inflated. I explained that I never asked the appraiser for specific values—she tendered them unilaterally. I never gave her financial incentives to inflate values, nor did I ever discuss inflating values with her.

But here's what the investigators didn't know: The lender had ordered review appraisals of each property from a third-party appraiser who was only available to the lender. In every single instance, the review appraisal confirmed the first appraiser's value. Additionally, the insurance company's appraised value exceeded both appraisal values.

This was conclusive evidence that I didn't influence the values. The market supported those numbers.

Point 3: Title Insurance Disclosure

They claimed title insurance companies weren't aware the properties were involved in two transactions. I had them pull the title commitments, which clearly showed both transactions were disclosed.

The evidence was right there in black and white.

I left that proffer session convinced I had shed substantial light on the allegations. The investigators even praised my recollection and knowledge of the transactions. They told me that out of over 200 interviews, I had disclosed things nobody else recalled.

They said they believed me.

I thought it was over. I thought truth and evidence would prevail.

I was wrong again.

THE ULTIMATUM

Months later, the FBI contacted me with an ultimatum: Plead guilty to charges, or they would indict me.

I considered it a bluff. After all, I'd met with them. I'd addressed every concern. They'd said they believed me. I had evidence, recordings, documents, independent appraisals, and title commitments.

So, I called their bluff. I refused to plead guilty to something I didn't do.

In December 2002, just before the statute of limitations expired on some charges, the federal government filed an 81-count indictment against my ex-wife, who wasn't even involved in the transactions, and me. It was also filed against my brother.

I later learned this was done as leverage to pressure me into taking a plea bargain.

THE INJUSTICE

This indictment changed my life and my view of the world.

Here's what was most telling: the lender, along with its officers and employees, was never charged, despite an audio recording of their confession, even though they orchestrated the entire structure, and even though they created the model that at least a dozen real estate professionals were using. That's when I realized only the African American real estate executives were being prosecuted. The only exception was the appraiser, who I can only assume was necessary to maintain the inflated-appraisal narrative.

But how? Everything on that tape was factual. I had shown them all the evidence: the appraisal reviews, the title commitments, and the independent legal opinions. They knew full well that I did not falsify any leases; in fact, I wasn't even in the country when the leases were created. I never imagined that this undisputed evidence would be completely ignored.

This couldn't really be happening.

Why would they indict my ex-wife and brother—people with no involvement in the alleged criminal conduct—while not indicting any of the many others who took part in identical transactions, worked on these deals, and did questionable things? Why was the government willing to portray the self-confessed orchestrators as victims?

What I learned was devastating: Perception is reality. And so much damage had been done to my reputation, my career, and my family that I couldn't see a way to recover. I will go to my grave believing that I was persecuted because I was a highly successful black man. I will never be able to shake that belief.

It was the lowest point of my life. I was only 31 years old when the indictment was finally handed down, and everything I'd built was crumbling. I eventually took a plea deal that dismissed all but two counts of the indictment in exchange for dropping the charges against my ex-wife and brother. It was the price I was ultimately willing to pay to move on with my life and to save theirs. It was a decision that left me with a cut so deep that it pains me to speak of it decades later. This memoir marks the first time I've spoken about it publicly.

THE SYSTEM

What made it even more surreal was how respectfully federal officials treated me throughout the process.

Probation officers and other federal employees who weren't even part of the investigation would come up to me and apologize. More than one told me they couldn't believe this was happening to me. Years later, a former prosecutor reached out to say that, inside their office, my case had been widely viewed as a miscarriage of justice. Others offered quiet encouragement, telling me I would land on my feet.

I came to understand that many of the federal employees I encountered genuinely respected me.

But none of that changed the outcome. In the end, I was still just another African American being processed by the system, another statistic, another life upended by prosecutorial overreach, inside a justice system that wasn't built to always care about actual justice. I'm not sure I'll ever fully understand how people can gain positions of power and then become so inhuman.

I have so much I can say about this period—about the pain, the betrayal, the injustice, the nights I couldn't sleep, the relationships that were destroyed, the reputation that was shattered.

But I want to focus on the comeback more than the setback.

Because that's where the real story is.

THE COMEBACK BEGINS

After my probation period ended, I didn't waste a single day.

I immediately hired an attorney to accompany me to the Tennessee Real Estate Commission to petition for the reinstatement of my license. I was prepared to go to a hearing and fight—to plead my case and do whatever it took.

But something unexpected happened.

While they searched for my records, someone at the commission remembered my case. I was told they would waive the hearing requirement. Instead, I could retake the exam, pass it, and have my license reinstated, which I did.

I had also successfully negotiated a non-debarment from federal programs. The doors weren't completely closed. I had a path forward.

But I knew the reality: If I were going to stage a comeback, I would have to work ten times harder and prove myself ten times more than ever before. After all, I had suffered damage to my name and reputation that I would spend the rest of my life trying to repair.

And that's exactly what I've done. Brick by brick. Day by day. Deal by deal.

WHAT THE FALL TAUGHT ME

That experience—as devastating as it was—taught me lessons I couldn't have learned any other way:

Lesson 1: The system isn't always just.

I had evidence. I had the truth on my side. I had done nothing wrong. And I was still indicted. That taught me that fairness isn't guaranteed, that justice isn't automatic, and that sometimes you must fight battles you shouldn't have to fight.

Lesson 2: Perception can override reality.

It didn't matter what the evidence showed. It didn't matter what the truth was. Once the narrative was set, once my name was in the headlines, the damage was done. That taught me the critical importance of reputation management and controlling your narrative before others control it for you.

Lesson 3: They will use the people you love as leverage.

Indicting my ex-wife and brother wasn't about justice—it was about pressure. It was about breaking me emotionally, so I'd take a plea. That taught me that when you're building something significant, you must protect not just yourself, but everyone connected to you.

Lesson 4: Your lowest point can become your launching pad.

At 31, I thought my life was over. I thought I'd never recover from this. But that rock bottom became the foundation I built everything else on. The P3 Group, the golf course, the Navy contract, the media empire, all of it was built by someone who had already survived his worst nightmare.

Lesson 5: Resilience isn't optional—it's everything.

I could have stayed down. I could have accepted defeat. I could have let that experience define the rest of my life. Instead, I decided it would refine me rather than define me. I proved that a setback, even one this devastating, was just a setup for a comeback.

THE REDEMPTION

Everything I've achieved since that indictment has been sweeter because of what I went through.

When I became the first African American owner of an 18-hole golf course in Arkansas and the Mid-South, that was redemption.

When I became the first minority Department of Defense contractor with a prime federal contract with the U.S. Navy Nuclear Power Training Unit, that was redemption.

When I built The P3 Group into the nation's leading African American-owned P3 firm, that was redemption.

When I received President Biden's Lifetime Achievement Award, that was redemption.

When my hometown named a street after me, that was redemption.

Every success, every "first," every barrier broken, it all means more because I know what it's like to lose everything and build it back from nothing.

THE MESSAGE

Here's what I want you to understand: Your greatest setback can become your greatest setup.

The thing that almost destroys you can become the thing that defines your strength, your character, and your ultimate success.

But only if you refuse to stay down.

I was 31 years old, facing 81 federal counts, watching my reputation destroyed, seeing my family dragged through hell, experiencing a level of injustice that still makes me angry when I think about it. But I got back up.

I rebuilt my license, my reputation, my business, and my life.

And I didn't just get back to where I was, I went far beyond it.

That's the power of resilience. That's the proof that your past doesn't have to determine your future. That's the evidence that a comeback is always possible if you're willing to do the work.

YOUR TURN

Maybe you're facing your own indictment right now. Maybe not a legal one, but a professional one. A financial one and a personal one.

Maybe you've been knocked down so hard that you're not sure you can get back up. Maybe people have written you off. Maybe you've written yourself off.

I'm here to tell you: Get back up.

The fight isn't over until you stop fighting. The story isn't finished until you stop writing. The comeback isn't impossible until you stop believing.

I've been where you are. I've felt that despair. I've experienced that injustice. I've faced that darkness.

And I'm here on the other side to tell you: You can make it through.

But you have to decide. You have to commit. You have to refuse to let your lowest point become your final chapter.

Because here's the truth: The world doesn't need another story about someone who got knocked down and stayed down. The world needs stories about people who got knocked down and got back up stronger, wiser, and more determined than ever.

That's the story I'm living. And that can be your story too.

So, whatever you're facing right now, whatever indictment, whatever setback, whatever injustice, decide right now that it will not be the end of your story.

Decide that it's going to be the turning point. The moment everything changed. The catalyst for your greatest comeback.

Because that's exactly what it can be—if you refuse to give up.

Now let's talk about the philosophy that's guided my approach to business and made breaking these barriers possible...

CHAPTER 6 –
THE P3 PHILOSOPHY

In the pursuit of the impossible dream, I discovered that the greatest achievements come not from going it alone, but from bringing together diverse resources toward a shared vision. The P3 philosophy became my vehicle for pursuing impossible dreams—creating partnerships that others said couldn't work and building developments that others said couldn't be done.

Let me introduce you to a concept that transformed my entire approach to business and became the foundation of my greatest success: Public-Private Partnerships, or P3s.

Now, I know what you might think: "Dee, that sounds complicated and technical. What does that have to do with me?"

Everything. Because the P3 philosophy isn't just about real estate development. It's about a mindset that can revolutionize how you approach any challenge, any opportunity, any goal.

At its core, the P3 philosophy is about bringing together diverse resources, strengths, and perspectives to create something greater than any single entity could create alone. It's about collaboration over competition. It's about a shared vision leading to shared success.

When I founded The P3 Group, I wasn't just starting another real estate development company. I was pioneering a model that skillfully combined the public and private sectors to create developments that served both business interests and community needs.

Think about that for a moment: What if your success didn't have to come at someone else's expense? What if you could build wealth while building communities? What if profit and purpose weren't opposing forces but complementary partners?

That's the P3 philosophy in action.

Here's how it works in practice: The public sector has resources, land, and a mandate to serve communities. The private sector has capital, expertise, and efficiency. Traditionally, these two worlds operated separately, often at odds.

I saw an opportunity to bring them together—to create partnerships where government needs, private capital, and ingenuity could align to build the infrastructure, housing, and facilities that communities desperately needed, while also creating profitable, sustainable businesses.

It was a win-win-win: the public sector completed projects efficiently. The private sector got profitable opportunities. And most importantly, communities got developments that served their needs.

I didn't just want to do deals. I wanted to create lasting places that benefit the communities they serve. I wanted to strengthen the socioeconomic fabric of neighborhoods that had been overlooked and underserved.

That's not just good business. That's a transformational business.

The P3 philosophy taught me something profound: The most sustainable success comes from creating value for everyone involved. When you structure opportunities so that all stakeholders benefit, you build something that lasts.

This is the opposite of the zero-sum mentality that dominates so much of business. You know the mindset I'm talking about: "For me to win, you have to lose." That's scarcity thinking, and it leads to short-term gains and long-term problems.

The P3 philosophy is abundance thinking: "When we all win, we all win bigger."

Let me give you a concrete example. When The P3 Group takes on a development project, we're not just thinking about our profit margin. We're thinking about job creation in the community. We're thinking about infrastructure improvements that will benefit residents for decades. We're thinking about the environmental impact. We're thinking about how this project fits into the larger vision for the community's future.

That comprehensive approach requires more work upfront. It requires more stakeholder engagement. It requires more complex negotiations. But the results are worth it.

We've overseen all phases of multi-million-dollar construction, infrastructure, water and sewer, and environmental projects for government and private-sector clients. Each of these projects has been a testament to what's possible when you bring diverse resources together and align them toward a common goal.

Let me give you a concrete example of the P3 philosophy in action—one that demonstrates how this model creates value for everyone involved while breaking new ground.

In 2019, The P3 Group entered into a contract with the city of West Memphis, Arkansas, to design, build, finance, and lease a district courthouse, two fire stations, and a police substation to the city. This wasn't just another development project. This was a comprehensive infrastructure initiative that the city desperately needed but couldn't execute through the traditional municipal financing and construction model because there was no approved public referendum.

Upon completion, these projects represented the first new municipal facilities in the city of West Memphis since 1974. Let that sink in—nearly 45 years without new municipal infrastructure. And they were the first municipal capital projects ever delivered via a public-private partnership in the state of Arkansas.

Another first for me. Another barrier broken. Another proof that the P3 model works.

This project exemplifies everything I've been talking about: We brought together public resources and private expertise to create infrastructure that the community needed. And we delivered results that transformed how the city could serve its residents.

That's the P3 philosophy: creating a real impact in the real world.

Here's another example that demonstrates the power of this model: The P3 Group designed, built, and leased the Bulldog Early Learning Academy to the Harrisburg, Illinois, community school district. This project represented the first K-12 school delivered under a public-private partnership in the state of Illinois.

Another first. Another barrier broken. Another proof that the P3 model can transform how communities access critical infrastructure.

Think about what this means: A school district that needed early learning facilities but couldn't secure traditional financing could provide high-quality educational infrastructure for its youngest students through a P3 partnership. We brought the expertise, the capital, and the execution. They brought the mission, the community's needs, and the long-term commitment.

Together, we created something that serves children and families—something that will impact generations of students in Harrisburg.

This is what I mean when I say the P3 philosophy creates value for everyone involved. The school district got the facilities it desperately needed. We built a sustainable business relationship. And most importantly, children in that community got access to quality early learning environments that will shape their entire educational journey.

These aren't just projects to me. They're proof that business can be a force for good, that profit and purpose can work together, that impossible dreams become reality when you bring the right partners together with the right vision.

Let me share one more example that demonstrates the P3 philosophy in action—this time in healthcare infrastructure serving underserved communities.

The P3 Group partnered with Lee County Cooperative Clinic under a design-build-finance agreement to deliver the new, state-of-the-art Olly Neal Community Health Center in Marianna, Arkansas. This nearly $12 million facility includes a drive-through pharmacy, radiology, dentistry, and comprehensive primary care services—critical healthcare access for a community that desperately needed it.

Here's where the P3 philosophy made this project possible: The Clinic secured grant funding, and the P3 Group helped obtain a HRSA Health Center Loan Guarantee (LGP), which guaranteed 80% of the loan's principal and interest on the loan. That guarantee was crucial—it dramatically reduced lender risk, making the project financeable in a way traditional approaches couldn't.

With this support in place, we secured a $10.6 million construction-to-permanent loan from Partners Bank to complete the project's capital stack. Think about the partnership coordination here: a community health clinic, federal loan guarantees, private banking, grant funding, and our design-build-finance expertise—all working together toward a common goal of delivering healthcare access to an underserved community.

The facility—now one of Arkansas's leading community healthcare centers—opened in October 2024. It isn't just a building. It's access to quality healthcare for families who've been underserved for generations. It's preventive care that will save lives. It's dental services for children who previously had no access. It's a drive-through pharmacy that makes medication accessible and convenient.

This is what I mean when I talk about embracing complexity and creating value for everyone involved. Most developers would have walked away from a healthcare project this intricate. But I saw an opportunity to serve a community that needed it, to prove that creative partnership structures can unlock possibilities that traditional approaches can't touch, and to demonstrate that business can be a force for good.

That's the P3 philosophy at its finest: bringing diverse resources together, navigating complexity, and creating lasting impact in communities.

Now, here's how you can apply the P3 philosophy to your own life and career, regardless of your industry:

First, identify complementary strengths. What do you bring to the table? What do others bring? How can these strengths combine to create something neither could create alone?

Maybe you're great at creative vision but weak on execution. Partner with someone who excels at implementation. Maybe you have technical expertise but lack business acumen. Find a partner who understands markets and finance.

The P3 philosophy says: Don't try to be everything. Be excellent at what you do, and partner with people who are excellent at what you're not.

Second, think beyond transactions to transformations. Don't just ask "How can I make money from this?" Ask "How can this create lasting value for everyone involved?"

When you shift from transactional thinking to transformational thinking, you unlock opportunities that others miss. You build relationships that endure. You create legacies that outlast you.

Third, embrace complexity. P3 deals are complex by nature. They involve multiple stakeholders, intricate regulations, and long-term commitments. Most people run from complexity. I run toward it.

Why? Because complexity creates barriers to entry. If something is easy, everyone does it, and the margins disappear. But if you can master complexity, you create a competitive moat that protects your position.

That expertise didn't come overnight. It came from embracing the complexity, studying it, mastering it, and then using it to create opportunities.

Fourth, focus on long-term relationships over short-term wins. The P3 model only works when all parties trust one another and commit to the project's long-term success.

I've built relationships with government officials, community leaders, and private investors that span decades. These relationships are built on a foundation of delivering on my commitments, operating with integrity, and always keeping the larger vision in mind.

In today's business world, where everyone is looking for the quick flip and the fast exit, long-term relationship building is a superpower.

Fifth, measure success by impact, not just income. Yes, The P3 Group is profitable. Yes, I've built personal wealth. But the metric I'm most proud of is the number of communities we've transformed, the number of jobs we've created, and the number of families whose lives are better because of the developments we've built.

That's the P3 philosophy: Profit with purpose. Wealth with impact. Success that serves.

I want to challenge you to think about your own work through this lens. How can you create partnerships that multiply your impact? How can you structure your business or career so that your success creates success for others?

This isn't just feel-good philosophy. It's strategic business thinking. When you create value for multiple stakeholders, you build a more resilient, more sustainable, more scalable enterprise.

The P3 Group has grown into the leading minority real estate development company that focuses exclusively on public-private partnerships. We didn't get there by accident. We got there by consistently applying this philosophy: bringing diverse resources together, aligning them toward shared goals, and creating value for everyone involved.

That's a model that works in any industry, market, or economy.

Whether you're in technology, healthcare, education, manufacturing, or any other field, the principles remain the same: Collaboration creates opportunities that competition cannot. Shared vision leads to shared success. Long-term relationships trump short-term transactions.

This is what the P3 philosophy taught me: You must share credit. In a traditional business model, the entrepreneur wants all the glory. In a P3 model, success is shared among multiple partners.

Some people struggle with that. Their ego needs to be the story's sole hero. But I learned early on that I'd rather have a smaller piece of massive success than 100% of a mediocre outcome.

When you're willing to share credit, you attract better partners. When you're willing to share success, you create bigger opportunities. When you're willing to share the spotlight, you build stronger teams.

The P3 philosophy is ultimately about abundance: There's enough success to go around. There's enough opportunity for everyone. There's enough wealth to be created for us all to win.

But it requires a shift in mindset. It requires moving from "me" to "we." It requires thinking systemically instead of individually. It takes patience to build something that lasts rather than grabbing quick wins.

The Mississippi Development Authority has recognized me as a business success story. I've been selected as a member of the Forbes Real Estate Council and the Forbes Business Council. I've received the Congressional Black Caucus Presidential Corporate Philanthropy Award.

These recognitions didn't come from being the smartest person in the room or the most aggressive dealmaker. They came from consistently applying the P3 philosophy: creating value for everyone, building lasting relationships, and focusing on transformational impact.

That's a philosophy that will serve you for a lifetime.

So, here's my challenge: Look at your current projects, goals, and challenges. How can you apply the P3 philosophy? Who could you partner with? What complementary strengths could you combine? How could you structure things so that everyone wins?

The answers to those questions might just unlock the breakthrough you've been searching for. The P3 philosophy taught me that impossible dreams become possible when you stop competing and start collaborating. Every major achievement in my career—from the Navy contract to building the nation's leading minority-owned P3 firm—was a pursuit of an impossible dream made real through strategic partnerships.

Let me pause here and tie together all the "firsts" I've achieved through this P3 philosophy—because each one represents an impossible dream that became reality:

Owning the golf course wasn't just a property acquisition; it was shattering a barrier in an industry where people who looked like me simply weren't present as owners.

I became the first minority Department of Defense contractor to hold a prime federal contract with the U.S. Navy Nuclear Training Unit. That opened doors for other minority contractors and proved that excellence transcends barriers.

The P3 Group delivered the first municipal capital projects under a public-private partnership in the state of Arkansas —the West Memphis courthouse, fire stations, and police substation.

We created the first municipally owned hotel in Arkansas history with the Courtyard by Marriott in Pine Bluff. This project required creating an entirely new governmental entity to make it legally possible.

The P3 Group also delivered Arkansas's first P3 community healthcare facilities, coroner's office, Veteran Affairs service center, and Museum, all of which provide critical services to Jefferson and Lee Counties.

We delivered the first K-12 school under a public-private partnership in the state of Illinois, the Bulldog Early Learning Academy in Harrisburg, providing critical early learning infrastructure that the district couldn't access through traditional financing.

And through all of this, The P3 Group became the nation's leading African American-owned public-private partnership real estate development firm.

Each of these "firsts" was someone's impossible dream. Each one required breaking through barriers that others accepted as permanent. Each one proved limitations are lies and that 'impossible' is just another word for 'untried'.

But here's what matters most: Each of these firsts created a pathway for others to follow. Each one expanded the realm of possibilities. Each one proved that the pursuit of the impossible dream isn't just about personal achievement—it's about showing others what's possible.

That's the power of the P3 philosophy combined with the relentless pursuit of impossible dreams. You don't just achieve success for yourself—you create a blueprint that others can follow and improve upon.

Now, let's see what happens when you apply this philosophy and things don't go according to plan—because they won't always...

CHAPTER 7 – RESILIENCE THROUGH ADVERSITY

Let me tell you something that nobody puts in their highlight reel: The path to success is paved with failures, setbacks, and moments when you seriously question whether you should keep going. Nobody posts on social media: The path to success is messy. It's filled with failures that sting, setbacks that break your heart, and moments when you lie awake at 3 AM wondering if you're fooling yourself, if you should just give up and get a regular job, if you're putting your family through all this struggle for nothing.

I've had deals fall apart at the last minute. I've had projects that seemed like sure things but collapsed. I've experienced financial pressures that kept me up at night. I've dealt with betrayals from people I trusted. I've had projects collapse that I'd invested months and sometimes years of work into. I've faced discrimination so blatant it took my breath away. I've been betrayed by people I trusted, people I considered friends. I've cried. I've doubted. I've questioned everything.

And I'm still here. Still building. Still growing. Still winning.

That's not because I'm special. It's because I learned the most important skill any entrepreneur can develop: Resilience.

Resilience isn't about never falling. It's about getting back up every single time. It's about treating setbacks as setups for comebacks. It's about refusing to let temporary defeats become permanent failures.

Over my 32-year career in real estate development, I've learned that adversity isn't the exception—it's the rule. If you're doing anything worthwhile, you'll face obstacles. The question isn't whether you'll encounter adversity. The question is, how will you respond when you do?

Let me share a truth that changed my perspective: Adversity is information. Every setback is telling you something. Every failure is teaching you something. Every obstacle reveals something about your strategy, your approach, or your preparation.

The key is to listen to what adversity is telling you, rather than just reacting emotionally.

When a deal falls through, I don't just get angry or discouraged. I analyze what happened. What did I miss? What could I have done differently? What does this teach me about future deals?

That analytical approach to adversity transforms it from something that defeats you into something that develops you.

Here's what I've learned about resilience: It's built in advance. You don't develop resilience in the moment of crisis. You develop it through the daily practices, the mindset work, and the support systems you build before adversity strikes.

I maintain my physical health through regular exercise. I maintain my mental health through meditation and reflection. I maintain my spiritual health through faith and purpose. I maintain my emotional health through strong relationships and a sense of community.

These aren't luxuries. They're necessities. Because when adversity hits, and it will hit, you need reserves to draw from.

I also learned to reframe how I think about challenges. Instead of asking, "Why is this happening to me?" I ask, "What is this preparing me for?"

That simple shift in perspective changes everything. Suddenly, adversity isn't random bad luck. It's targeted training for the next level of success you're about to reach.

When I faced the challenge of being the first minority contractor in certain spaces, I could have focused on how unfair it was, how much harder I had to work, how many more obstacles I faced. And yes, all of that was true.

But I focused on how this adversity was making me sharper, stronger, and more prepared. I saw it as a competitive advantage in disguise. While my competitors were coasting, I was forged in the fire.

That's the mindset that builds resilience: Adversity isn't happening to you. It's happening for you.

Let me talk about a specific type of adversity that every entrepreneur faces: Financial pressure. There have been times in my career when cash flow was tight, when payroll was coming due, and receivables were delayed, when I had to make tough decisions about where to allocate limited resources.

Those moments test you. They reveal what you're made of. They force you to be creative, to hustle harder, to find solutions where none seem to exist.

Financial adversity teaches you to be a better business operator. It forces you to tighten your systems, to improve your processes, and to eliminate waste. Companies that never face financial pressure often become bloated and inefficient.

The adversity makes you lean, mean, and efficient.

Let me share a specific example of resilience in action—a project that tested every ounce of determination and commitment I had.

As I mentioned, the P3 Group entered into a contract with the city of West Memphis, Arkansas, to design, build, finance, and lease a district courthouse, two fire stations, and a police substation to the city. What I didn't share then is what happened shortly after we signed the agreement.

COVID-19 hit.

Suddenly, we faced obstacles no one could have predicted. Supply chains collapsed. Construction materials became scarce or prohibitively expensive. Workers were getting sick. Safety protocols had to be completely reimagined. The entire world was in chaos, and we were undertaking major infrastructure projects.

I won't lie to you—there were moments when I wondered if we could pull it off. There were nights when the stress felt overwhelming. There were days when it seemed like every problem we solved revealed two new problems.

But we had made a commitment to the city of West Memphis. Those weren't just buildings we were constructing—they were essential services that the community needed. A courthouse where justice would be served. Fire stations that would save lives. A police substation that would protect residents.

We couldn't let a pandemic stop us from delivering on that commitment.

So, we adapted. We got creative with sourcing materials. We implemented rigorous safety protocols. We communicated constantly with all stakeholders. We problem-solved in real-time. We refused to use the pandemic as an excuse.

And I wasn't doing this alone. My Chief Operating Officer, Grandon Gray, was right there with me every step of the way. Grandon's business development skills are the perfect complement to what I bring to the company. While I focus on execution and vision, he focuses on relationships and operations. That partnership has been invaluable to The P3 Group's success.

But during COVID-19, that partnership was tested like never before. It felt like we were in the literal trenches together—managing projects that were constantly threatened by supply chain disruptions, maintaining relationships with nervous stakeholders, and managing expectations when nobody knew what tomorrow would bring. We were on calls at all hours, solving problems in real-time, supporting each other when the pressure felt overwhelming.

That's when you discover what your team is really made of. That's when partnerships prove their worth. Grandon and I didn't just survive that crisis—we grew stronger through it.

And we delivered on time. Meeting all specifications and creating infrastructure that will serve that community for generations. And we did it while providing twelve million dollars in capital to design and construct these facilities.

That's resilience. That's what it means to honor your commitments, no matter what obstacles arise. That's what separates those who achieve the impossible from those who give up when things get hard.

But our response to COVID-19 went beyond construction projects. When the pandemic hit, local governments, healthcare facilities, prisons, and state agencies were desperate for Personal Protective Equipment. Lives were on the line, and the supply chain was in chaos.

The P3 Group was asked to help, and we moved quickly. We identified and vetted manufacturers in China and Mexico that could meet the varying specifications required by different organizations. This wasn't our typical work, but it was what our communities needed.

We supplied dozens of agencies with essential items—masks, gowns, goggles, thermometers, shoe covers, and COVID-19 testing kits. Ultimately, we delivered over twenty million dollars in PPE.

But here's what made this work challenging: The market was flooded with pop-up vendors who took upfront payments and then disappeared, leaving agencies without the equipment their workers desperately needed. Trust was broken. People were scared.

So, we implemented a different model. We secured and delivered the PPE first, then had the agency inspect it. Payment wasn't due until 72 hours after receiving the receipt. This significantly reduced the risk for our partners and restored accountability during an unprecedented crisis.

The work was urgent and high-stakes. The health, safety, and lives of essential workers—nurses, doctors, corrections officers, first responders— depended on us getting reliable PPE delivered fast. We weren't just moving products. We were protecting the people who were protecting all of us.

That's what resilience looks like when you expand your vision beyond your core business to serve your community in crisis.

And while we were managing PPE procurement and the West Memphis construction projects, we simultaneously took on another massive challenge. The P3 Group designed, built, and leased a community health department, coroner's office, and Veterans Affairs service center and museum for Jefferson County, Arkansas—projects that required us to provide eighteen million dollars in capital.

Think about what we were juggling: sourcing and delivering twenty million dollars in PPE to keep essential workers safe, completing municipal facilities in West Memphis, and now designing and constructing health infrastructure during a health crisis. Between the West Memphis projects requiring twelve million dollars in capital, the Jefferson County facilities requiring eighteen million, and the twenty million in PPE we were procuring and delivering, we were managing over fifty million dollars in commitments during the height of COVID-19. The uncertainty was overwhelming. Nobody knew how long the pandemic would last, what the economic impact would be, or whether any of these projects could even continue safely.

We weren't just building standard facilities. We were building health infrastructure during a health crisis. We had to incorporate COVID-19 responses in real-time as we designed and constructed these buildings.

We installed negative-pressure HVAC systems to prevent airborne contamination. We built a decontamination unit at the coroner's office— something that wasn't even in the original plans but became essential as we understood the pandemic's impact. We created a drive-through COVID-19 testing facility at the health unit so the community could access testing safely.

Think about the scope of what we were managing simultaneously: vetting international PPE manufacturers and delivering critical supplies to keep essential workers alive, adapting construction designs on the fly for West Memphis, and now incorporating real-time COVID-19 responses to health facilities for Jefferson County. We were responding to a crisis that was evolving daily, managing over $50 million in commitments, and maintaining our commitment to deliver quality infrastructure across it all.

Even during a pandemic, we secured a one-million-dollar naming rights sponsorship from Simmons Bank for the Jefferson County projects. The health unit and Veterans Affairs Service Center both feature a Simmons Bank lobby. That shows the power of relationships, the value of reputation, and the importance of maintaining excellence even in a crisis.

These projects exemplify resilience at every level. We didn't just survive the pandemic—we served our community during its greatest time of need. We created facilities that literally saved lives during COVID-19 and will continue serving these communities for generations.

That's what resilience looks like in action: Not just enduring adversity, but using it as an opportunity to serve, to innovate, and to prove what you're capable of when everything is on the line.

I also learned the importance of having a strong support system during times of adversity. As a proud member of Kappa Alpha Psi Fraternity, I have been able to lean on that brotherhood throughout so many of my business endeavors. I have fraternity brothers in every imaginable leadership position—people who've walked similar paths and can offer perspective when I'm too close to a problem to see clearly.

You cannot build resilience in isolation. You need people who believe in you when you're struggling to believe in yourself. You need people who've overcome similar challenges and can show you it's possible. You need people who will tell you the truth even when it's hard to hear.

Build that support system before you need it. Because when adversity strikes, you won't have the energy to build relationships from scratch.

Here's another key to resilience: Maintain perspective. In the moment, every setback feels catastrophic. Every failure feels final. Every obstacle feels insurmountable.

But when you look back on your life, you'll realize that the things that seemed like disasters at the time were actually redirections toward something better.

I've had deals that I desperately wanted to fall through, only to have better opportunities emerge shortly after. I've had partnerships that ended painfully, only to realize later that they were holding me back from my true potential.

I've had failures that felt devastating in the moment but taught me lessons that led to massive successes later.

Time gives you perspective. But you can speed up that perspective by consciously choosing to see setbacks as setups.

Let me share something practical about building resilience: Celebrate small wins. When you're going through adversity, it's easy to focus only on what's going wrong. But there are always things going right, even in the darkest times.

I make it a practice to acknowledge progress, no matter how small—closed a small deal when you were hoping for a big one? Celebrate it. Made it through a tough week without giving up? Acknowledge that. Learned a valuable lesson from a failure? Honor that growth.

These small celebrations build momentum. They remind you that you're moving forward even when it doesn't feel like it. They fuel the resilience you need to keep going.

I also learned to control what I can control and release what I can't. So much of the adversity we face comes from trying to control things beyond our sphere of influence.

I can't control the economy. I can't control discrimination. I can't control other people's decisions. But I can control my effort, attitude, preparation, and response.

When I focus my energy on what I can control, I feel empowered. When I waste energy on what I can't control, I feel victimized.

Resilience comes from choosing empowerment over victimhood, every single day.

Don't just survive adversity—use it. Every challenge you overcome makes you more credible, more capable, and more confident.

When I speak at conferences now, I don't just share my successes. I share my failures and how I overcame them. That's what people connect with. That's what inspires them. That's what gives them hope they can overcome their own challenges.

Your adversity becomes your authority. Your struggles become your story. Your resilience becomes your reputation.

I've received President Biden's Lifetime Achievement Award. I've been recognized by Fortune magazine and the Congressional Black Caucus. But the recognition that means the most is when someone tells me, "Your story gave me the courage to keep going when I wanted to quit."

That's the power of resilience: It's contagious. When people see you overcome adversity, it permits them to believe they can overcome theirs.

Here's something I've learned about overcoming obstacles: You can't do it alone. I don't care how talented, smart, or determined you are—you need a team.

Success is a team sport. The obstacles you'll face are too big, too complex, too multifaceted for any one person to handle alone.

I've built incredible teams across all my ventures. In real estate, in media, in fashion, in spirits—every successful project has resulted from talented people working together toward a shared vision.

But here's the key: You must be consistent. Your team needs to know that you'll show up every day with the same commitment, the same standards, and the same vision. They need to know that when obstacles arise, you won't panic or quit. They need to know that you're in it for the long haul.

That consistency builds trust. And trust allows teams to perform at the highest level.

I've maintained that consistency for over 32 years. My teams know I'll deliver on my commitments. They know that I'm going to support them. They know I'll maintain our standards no matter what challenges we face.

That consistency has allowed me to attract and keep exceptional talent. People want to work with someone they can count on, someone who's going to be there through the ups and downs, someone who's committed to excellence no matter what.

Build that reputation for consistency, and you'll never lack for talented people who want to be part of your team.

So, here's my challenge: Whatever adversity you're facing right now, decide that it will not defeat you. Decide that it's going to develop you. Decide that you're going to use it as fuel for your next level of success.

Analyze what it's teaching you. Lean on your support system. Maintain perspective. Celebrate small wins. Control what you can control. And most importantly, keep moving forward.

Because resilience isn't about never getting knocked down, it's about always getting back up.

And every time you get back up, you get stronger. Every time you overcome adversity, you build confidence. Every time you push through when it would be easier to quit, you prove to yourself what you're capable of.

That's how champions are made, not in the moments of easy victory, but in the moments of difficult perseverance.

You are more resilient than you know. You are stronger than you think. You can overcome more than you can imagine.

But you'll only discover that resilience by facing adversity and refusing to let it win.

So, bring on the challenges. Bring on the obstacles. Bring on the setbacks. Because every single one of them is just another opportunity to prove what you're made of.

Resilience keeps you pursuing the impossible dream when everyone else has given up. It's what separates those who achieve the impossible from those who accept defeat. Every setback I've overcome was just another step in the pursuit of my impossible dream.

Now let's talk about how to take that resilience and apply it to building multiple streams of success...

CHAPTER 8 –
DIVERSIFY YOUR VISION

Why limit your pursuit of the impossible dream to just one arena? This chapter is about expanding your vision across multiple domains, proving that impossible dreams aren't confined to a single industry or a single achievement. My journey from real estate to media to fashion to spirits, each was its own impossible dream pursued and achieved.

Here's a question that will change how you think about success: Why limit yourself to being great at just one thing?

I'm the founder and CEO of The P3 Group. I could have stopped there. I could have said, "This is my lane, and I'm staying in it."

But that's not how I'm built. And if you're reading this book, that's probably not how you're built either.

I'm also an award-winning producer, director, writer, and author. I'm a talk show host. I own a golf course. I run a film production company. I host an internationally ranked podcast. I have a luxury clothing line. I launched a tequila brand. I have operated a yacht charter company with a 100-foot luxury yacht.

When I tell people about all these ventures, they often ask, "How do you manage all of that? Aren't you spreading yourself too thin?"

My answer: I'm not spreading myself thin. I'm expanding my impact.

There's a difference.

Diversification isn't about doing a bunch of random things. It's about building multiple expressions of your core vision and values. It's about building a portfolio of ventures that reinforce one another and compound your success.

Let me explain the philosophy behind my diversification strategy: Everything I do is connected to a central brand—self Made. That brand represents a mindset, a lifestyle, a commitment to excellence and self-determination.

Real estate development? That's Self Made in action—building wealth and communities from the ground up.

Media production? That's Self Made storytelling—sharing narratives that inspire others to create their own success.

One venture that really embodies this philosophy is my work in local media: the Clarksdale Advocate, which I rebranded as the Mississippi Delta Advocate in January 2026.

I launched a local newspaper because I saw a gap that needed to be filled. You see, most media focus on the negative—the crime, the problems, the failures. And yes, those things exist. But they're not the whole story.

I looked at my community, and I saw incredible things happening. I saw people overcoming obstacles. I saw businesses succeeding. I saw young people achieving. I saw neighbors helping neighbors. I saw positive stories that deserved to be told.

But nobody was telling them.

So, I created the Clarksdale Advocate as a nonprofit to highlight the uplifting stories, positive developments, and good things happening in our community that the mainstream media ignored.

It wasn't just about running a newspaper. It was about changing the narrative. It was about showing people in the community that there's more to their story than what the evening news reports show. It was about celebrating success, highlighting achievements, and inspiring others through positive examples.

The Advocate became a platform for community voices, for local businesses, for success stories that needed to be shared. It showed me the power of the media to shape perception, inspire action, and build community pride.

That experience taught me that media isn't just entertainment—it's a tool for transformation. It's a way to amplify positive messages, celebrate achievements, and inspire others to pursue their own dreams.

That's why I later expanded into Self Made Entertainment, Self-Made TV, and my podcast.

Self-Made Entertainment isn't just a production company—it's a complete media ecosystem. We produce television shows, and we even have a record label.

Let me give you a sense of the scope of this media work, because it demonstrates what I mean by bringing excellence to everything you do.

I've produced over 200 episodes of PBS television as a talk-show host and executive producer. That's not a side project—that's a substantial body of work that reaches communities across the country, creating platforms for important conversations and inspiring stories.

But I didn't stop at television. I also create documentaries that are distributed across major streaming platforms, including Prime Video, Apple TV, and Tubi. These aren't vanity projects; they're films that tackle important subjects and tell stories that need to be told.

My documentary credits include "No House to Morehouse" with Dr. Lester McCorn, exploring the transformative power of education to take you from poverty to prosperity. "Tiger Run" with Coach Prime, documenting his leadership and impact at Jackson State University. "Foundling" with Judge Joseph Wood, examining the journey of a child abandoned in the winter streets of Chicago at birth. "Death at the Faucet" with the Southern Poverty Law Center and the Poor People's Campaign, investigating environmental injustice. "Death at the Faucet II" with Congressman Bennie Thompson and Dr. Pam Gary, continuing that critical work. And "Grave Injustice" with Marla Dickerson, exposing systemic inequities.

Each of these documentaries represents a commitment to using media as a force for good, to shine a light on important issues, and to give voice to those who need to be heard.

This body of work earned me membership in the Producers Guild of America—not as an honorary member, but as someone who's done the work, produced content to the highest professional standards, and contributed meaningfully to the industry.

And this work has been recognized with multiple awards. Those awards didn't come from celebrity status or connections; they came from excellence in storytelling, production quality, and meaningful content.

Yes, a record label. Because entertainment is about more than just one medium, it's about creating content across multiple platforms, reaching audiences in different ways, and telling stories through various formats. We create content that aligns with our values, which tells the stories we want to tell, that serves the audiences we want to reach.

And we do it on our terms, on our timeline, with our standards.

The record label allows us to support artists, to create music that inspires, and to add another dimension to the Self Made brand.

All of this connects back to that early lesson from the Clarksdale Advocate: Media is powerful. Storytelling matters. And when you control your own platforms, you control your own narrative.

Fashion? That's Self Made style—expressing success through how you present yourself.

Tequila? That's Self Made celebration—enjoying the fruits of your labor. And let's talk about the real story behind Self Made Dee Brown, CEO of Sipping Tequila, because it perfectly illustrates strategic diversification.

When I entered the spirits industry, people thought I was crazy. "You're a real estate developer," they said. "What do you know about tequila?"

And they were right—I didn't know much about tequila. But I knew about branding. I knew about quality. I knew about creating premium products. And I knew I could learn what I didn't know.

I wanted complete control over my brand. I didn't want to license my name to someone else's product. I wanted to own it, control it, and ensure it met my standards.

So, I went to Mexico. I learned about tequila production. I learned that premium 100% agave tequila must be produced and bottled in Mexico; that's not just tradition; that's regulation. I learned about the different types: blanco, reposado, añejo, extra añejo, each aged differently and with distinct characteristics.

I learned that making great tequila takes time. The agave plants take years to mature before they can even be harvested. Then there's the production process, the aging, the refinement.

But I was willing to invest that time because I was committed to excellence.

Before I launched, I did something crucial: I tested it. I brought together family, friends, and business associates for blind taste tests. I didn't tell them it was my product. I just had them taste different tequilas and give me honest feedback.

And you know what? My tequila consistently won those blind comparisons. People preferred it over brands that cost twice as much and had been on the market for decades.

That validation told me I had something special.

I wanted to create a tequila that represented the Self Made brand. Premium quality. Sophisticated. Something you'd be proud to serve, proud to gift, proud to celebrate with.

When we launched Self Made Dee Brown CEO Sipping Tequila in spring 2023, it wasn't just another celebrity spirits brand. It was a carefully crafted product I oversaw from production to bottling, that met the highest standards, that represented everything the Self Made brand stands for.

And the response has been incredible, not because of aggressive marketing, but because the product delivers on its promise.

That's the lesson: When you diversify, don't just add random ventures. Add ventures that extend your brand, which leverage your strengths, and that meet the same standards of excellence as everything else you do.

The yacht? That's Self Made lifestyle: living the dream you worked so hard to achieve. See how it all connects? Each venture isn't a distraction from my core business. It's an extension of my core brand.

That's strategic diversification.

Here's why diversification matters: It creates resilience. When one industry faces challenges, you have other revenue streams. When one venture hits a plateau, another is growing. When one market contracts, another expands.

I learned this lesson during economic downturns. While some of my competitors who were solely focused on real estate struggled, I had media ventures, fashion, and other businesses that continued to generate revenue and maintain my brand presence.

Diversification isn't just smart business. It's a survival strategy.

But here's the key: You must diversify from a position of strength, not weakness. Don't start a new venture because your current business is failing. Start it because your current business is succeeding and you're ready to expand your impact.

I didn't launch Self Made Entertainment because The P3 Group was struggling. I launched it because The P3 Group was thriving and I had the resources, credibility, and vision to expand into media.

Each new venture should build on the success of previous ones, not distract from them. Let me tell you about another venture that perfectly illustrates this: my yacht charter business.

I had operated a 100-foot luxury yacht named Self Made. Now, some people might see that as just an extravagant toy. But it was a strategic business asset that served multiple purposes.

First, it was a charter business. We offered luxury yacht experiences, and it generated revenue as a legitimate business venture.

Second, it was a branding tool. The yacht embodied the Self Made lifestyle. It was a physical manifestation of what's possible when you build from nothing. It represented the celebration of success, the enjoyment of the fruits of your labor.

Third, it was a business development tool. I hosted clients, partners, and potential collaborators on the yacht. There's something about being out on the water, away from offices and distractions, which creates space for meaningful conversations and relationship building.

But here's what really struck me about that yacht: It was bigger than the house I grew up in.

Think about that for a moment. I went from a childhood home where we struggled to make ends meet, with my mother working multiple jobs to keep us fed and housed, to owning a yacht larger than that entire house.

That's not just success. That's transformation. That's proof that where you start doesn't determine where you finish.

In many ways, Self-Made was the crown jewel of the Self Made brand— the ultimate symbol of what's possible when you refuse to accept limitations.

This is what happened to Self-Made, because it taught me something profound about resilience and loss.

In October 2023, I attended a charity event at Jackson State University, where the University unveiled The P3 Group's name on the major donor's wall in the center of campus. It was a wonderful evening hosted by the JSU Development Foundation—a celebration of giving back and supporting education.

Later that night, when I returned to my hotel room, I received a phone call that shook my family to the core. Around 10:30 p.m. Central time, my first mate from the motor yacht Self Made called me in a panic and asked if I had heard from the marina. I told her I hadn't. She said the marina had called her and that she was heading there, but she had been told Self Made was engulfed in flames.

The news was devastating. Self-Made wasn't just a business venture or an asset on a balance sheet. It was our home. It was a 100-foot luxury yacht with seven bedrooms and seven-and-a-half baths, maintained by a full-time crew. My family and I often lived onboard. It was one of our homes. Getting that call felt no different from being told your house was on fire.

Self-Made was a total loss. The crown jewel of the Self Made brand—gone.

It deeply affected my family and the crew who had cared for her. Thankfully, no one was on board, and there were no injuries. But the emotional impact was profound. It wasn't just losing a yacht; it was losing a home, a symbol of everything I'd built, a piece of the dream I'd worked so hard to achieve.

The experience drained my passion for yachting. I couldn't imagine replacing Self Made. She was irreplaceable, not just as a vessel, but as what she represented.

I believe one reason I moved so quickly on the golf course deal was that I was searching for something to fill the void left by the loss of Self Made. I was working through the loss psychologically, and I needed a new challenge, a new achievement, a new symbol of what's possible.

That's what adversity does, it redirects you. Sometimes painfully. Sometimes in ways you don't expect. But if you let it, it can push you toward opportunities you might not have pursued otherwise.

Losing Self Made taught me that even when you lose something precious, you keep building. You keep creating. You keep moving forward. Because the dream isn't contained in any single achievement or possession—it's in the relentless pursuit itself.

This is how I think about diversification: I look for opportunities that leverage my existing strengths, relationships, and reputation while allowing me to develop new capabilities.

When I started my podcast "The Sky's the Limit: Beyond the Deal" in collaboration with Forbes Books, I wasn't starting from scratch. I brought my business expertise, my network of high-level contacts, and my reputation as a successful entrepreneur. But I also had to develop new skills in media production, interviewing, and content creation.

That's the sweet spot: Leverage what you have while stretching into what you want to become.

This same principle of leveraging existing strengths while developing new capabilities took me from hosting a podcast with Forbes to hosting two award-winning talk shows with WTVP PBS.

That discovery led me to television. I didn't just want to share my story—I wanted to create platforms where other people's stories could inspire and educate. So, I developed two talk shows with WTVP PBS—"Self Made" and "#HBCYou"—and both have won awards for their storytelling quality and the value they bring to audiences.

Here's what made this transition successful: my ability to help others articulate their journeys, ask the right questions, and draw out insights that audiences could apply to their own lives. It wasn't just about me being on camera; it was about creating space for meaningful conversations that could change people's perspectives and inspire them to action.

This became an important part of building my brand. I wasn't just known as a successful real estate developer anymore. I was becoming known as someone who could help others share their knowledge, someone who created platforms for important conversations, someone who understood that success is amplified when you help others succeed.

Each venture makes me more well-rounded, more capable, more valuable.

Diversification keeps you intellectually engaged. After 32 years in real estate development, I could do many aspects of that business in my sleep. That's great for efficiency, but it's terrible for growth.

When I'm working on a television show, I'm challenged in new ways. When I'm developing a tequila brand, I'm learning new industries. When I'm operating a yacht charter business, I'm solving different problems.

That constant learning keeps me sharp. It keeps me excited. It keeps me growing.

And growth is what life is all about.

Now, let me give you some practical guidance on how to diversify your own vision:

First, identify your main strengths. What are you genuinely excellent at? What do people consistently come to you for? What creates the most value in your current work?

For me, it's vision, deal-making, branding, and storytelling. Those main strengths show up in every venture I pursue, even though the industries are different.

Second, look for adjacent opportunities. What industries or markets are close to what you're already doing? What skills have you developed that could be applied in new contexts?

Real estate development and media production might seem unrelated, but they both involve storytelling, project management, and bringing together diverse teams to create something valuable. The skills transfer more than you might think.

Third, test before you fully commit. I didn't immediately invest millions in my tequila brand. I started small, tested the market, learned the industry, and then scaled up as I gained confidence and competence.

Too many people make the mistake of going all-in on a new venture before they've validated the concept. Test, learn, adjust, then scale.

Fourth, build teams. I can't manage every detail of every business I own. That's impossible. But I can build strong teams, set clear vision and values, and create systems that allow these businesses to operate without requiring my constant attention.

Diversification only works if you're willing to delegate and trust others to execute your vision.

Fifth, maintain brand coherence. All of my ventures connect back to the Self Made brand. They reinforce each other. They tell a consistent story about who I am and what I stand for.

If I suddenly launched a discount retail chain or a fast-food franchise, it would confuse my brand. Not because those businesses are bad, but because they don't align with the premium, excellence-focused brand I've built.

Make sure your diversification strengthens your brand rather than diluting it.

Here's another key to successful diversification: do whatever you do with excellence. Don't just add ventures to say you have them. Add ventures that you're committed to making world-class.

Half-hearted diversification is worse than no diversification. It drains your resources, damages your reputation, and distracts from your core business.

But strategic, excellent diversification? That's how you build an empire.

Diversification has made me more interesting. When I'm in a room with other real estate developers, I can talk about media production, fashion, spirits, and yachting. That makes me memorable. It creates conversation. It opens doors.

It's also made me more resilient. Economic downturns affect different industries differently. Having multiple revenue streams means I'm never completely dependent on any single market.

And perhaps most importantly, it's made my life more fulfilling. I'm not just doing the same thing day after day, year after year. I'm constantly exploring new challenges, learning new skills, meeting new people, and creating new value.

That's what keeps me energized after 32 years in business.

So, here's my challenge to you: What's the next expression of your vision? What adjacent opportunities could you explore? What new venture could leverage your existing strengths while developing new capabilities?

Don't limit yourself to one lane. Don't accept the box that others try to put you in. Don't believe that you have to choose between being a specialist and being diverse.

You can be both. You can be deeply excellent in multiple domains. You can build a portfolio of ventures that reinforce each other and compound your success.

That's not spreading yourself thin. That's expanding your impact.

And the world needs your expanded impact. Diversifying your vision means pursuing multiple impossible dreams simultaneously. Each venture I've built—The P3 Group, Self Made Entertainment, the golf course, the fashion line, the tequila brand—was someone's impossible dream. I just refused to limit myself to pursuing only one.

Now let's talk about how to ensure that all this success matters—by giving back and lifting others as you rise...

CHAPTER 9 –
GIVE BACK TO RISE HIGHER

The pursuit of the impossible dream isn't just about personal achievement—it's about lifting others as you rise. This chapter is about how giving back transforms your impossible dream from a selfish pursuit into a legacy that outlasts you.

Let me share something that took me years to understand fully: True success isn't measured by what you accumulate. It's measured by what you contribute. True success isn't about the size of your bank account or the number of properties you own. It's about the lives you touch. The people you help—the hope you create. I had to learn this lesson because, for a long time, I was chasing the wrong things, trying to prove my worth through accumulation. But that never filled the emptiness. What fills it is knowing that my work matters to someone beyond myself.

I could fill this chapter with stories about deals I've closed, buildings I've developed, and wealth I've created. And yes, those things matter. But they're not what I'm most proud of.

What I'm most proud of is the Brown Foundation Community Development Corporation. It's the communities we've transformed. It's the young entrepreneurs I've mentored. It's the doors I've opened for others. It's the legacy I'm building that will outlast me. When I think about what I'm truly proud of, it's not the deals, the buildings, or the wealth. It's the young entrepreneur who tells me my mentorship changed their life. It's the families living in quality housing that the Brown Foundation helped create. It's the students attending college because of our housing developments. It's knowing that long after I'm gone, the Brown Foundation will still serve communities, still creating opportunities, still giving people hope.

That's what giving back is about: Creating impact that extends beyond your lifetime. And for me, this commitment to giving back is deeply personal. It's rooted in a promise I made to honor my mother's memory.

My mother lived in poverty as a child. As an adult, she worked multiple jobs and sacrificed everything for her children.

In August 2023, my mother passed away after a lengthy battle with breast cancer. In her final days, she faced her situation with remarkable courage and clarity, choosing not to be sedated by pain medication even as her body grew weaker and her pain became immense.

I was with her at the end and witnessed the profound transition from life to death. Seeing her strength and the reality of that moment deeply affected me, changing how I understand life, loss, and what truly matters.

Her strength reminded me how often people let fear and failure steal their opportunities. It also made me realize that time is finite, and we must live fully, seize each opportunity, and take nothing for granted.

That breaks my heart. But it also fuels my purpose.

All the wealth I've built, all the success I've achieved—none of it could save her. That's a hard truth I carry with me every day. But what I can do is honor her memory by helping other mothers, other families, other people who are struggling the way she struggled. I can make sure her legacy of sacrifice and strength lives on through the lives we touch and the communities we serve.

Every time the Brown Foundation helps a family find affordable housing, I'm honoring my mother. Every time we support education programs that give young people opportunities, I'm honoring my mother. Every time we invest in community development that lifts people out of poverty, I'm honoring my mother.

She taught me that your circumstances don't define you. She showed me that hard work and integrity matter more than advantages. She demonstrated you can maintain your dignity and your values even in the most difficult situations.

Now I get to take those lessons and multiply them through the Foundation's work. I get to ensure that her struggles weren't in vain. I get to create the opportunities for others that she never had for herself.

That's not charity. That's legacy. That's love in action.

My mother came from nothing and built a family on faith, hard work, and unwavering determination. She showed me what's possible when you refuse to let circumstances defeat you. Now, through the Brown Foundation, I'm helping other families write their own success stories—stories my mother would be proud of.

And speaking of my mother and my hometown, this is something that moved me deeply.

In June 2025, two years after my mother's passing, my hometown of Clarksdale, Mississippi, honored me by naming a street in my childhood neighborhood after me. The street where I grew up playing football and kickball, the street where I dreamed my first dreams, where I ran with my friends, where I learned what community meant, was renamed "Dee Brown Lane."

I can't fully express what that meant to me. To go from being a kid on that street, wondering if I'd ever escape poverty, to having that same street bear my name—that's not just an honor. That's a testament to what's possible. That's proof that you can come from nothing and still make something of yourself. That's validation that the journey matters, that the struggle has meaning, that coming back to lift up your community is what success is about.

When I stood on Dee Brown Lane for the first time after the renaming, I thought about my mother. I wished so deeply that she could have been there to see it. I thought about all the times she walked those streets, working multiple jobs, sacrificing everything. I thought about the young Dee Brown who played on that street, dreaming of a better life but not yet knowing how to get there.

And I thought about the young people in Clarksdale today who are walking on Dee Brown Lane, who might see that street sign and think, "If he made it out and came back to give back, maybe I can too."

This is what honor really means. It's not about me. It's about showing the next generation that their dreams are valid, that their hometown believes in them, that success doesn't mean forgetting where you came from—it means remembering and giving back.

I approach the world of charity with a firm conviction: One's ability to positively influence society—rather than just achieving financial gain—is what truly defines success. It isn't just a nice philosophy. It's a fundamental truth that I've built my entire career around.

I learned that giving back isn't separate from building wealth. It's integral to it. When you invest in your community, you're not just being charitable. You're creating an ecosystem that supports sustainable success for everyone, including yourself.

Think about it: When I develop properties through The P3 Group, I'm not just building structures. I'm creating jobs for local workers. I'm improving infrastructure that benefits entire neighborhoods. I'm increasing property values for existing homeowners. I'm creating spaces where businesses can thrive, and families can flourish.

That's not charity. That's enlightened self-interest. Because when communities thrive, businesses thrive. When people have opportunities, they create value. When neighborhoods improve, everyone benefits.

The Brown Foundation Community Development Corporation is committed to improving communities, advancing education, and nourishing the aspirations of future generations. We don't just write checks to causes. We invest strategically in initiatives that create lasting change.

Education programs that give young people skills and opportunities. Community development projects that revitalize neighborhoods. Entrepreneurship initiatives that help others start and grow businesses. These investments pay dividends that compound over generations.

But let me be clear about something: Giving back isn't just about money. It's about time, expertise, and access. I mentor young entrepreneurs. I speak at conferences and share what I've learned. I serve on boards where I can influence policy and create opportunities. I write articles that share insights with people I'll never meet. I'm writing this book to reach people who might never have access to me personally.

That's giving back through knowledge transfer. And in many ways, it's more valuable than financial contributions.

Here's why giving back is so important: It keeps you grounded. When you're building wealth and achieving success, it's easy to lose touch with the struggles that most people face. It's easy to forget where you came from. It's easy to become isolated in a bubble of privilege.

Giving back forces you to stay connected to real people facing real challenges. It reminds you why you're doing what you're doing. It keeps your purpose clear and your motivation pure.

I've received the Congressional Black Caucus Presidential Corporate Philanthropy Award and President Biden's Lifetime Achievement Award. These honors recognize not just my business success, but my commitment to using that success to create opportunities for others.

That's the kind of recognition that means something. Because it's not about what I've achieved for myself, it's about what I've enabled for others.

Here is a practical framework for giving back that I've developed over the years:

First, give strategically. Don't just respond to every request that comes your way. Identify causes and communities that align with your values and where you can make the most impact.

For me, that's education, entrepreneurship, and community development. Those are areas where I have expertise, passion, and the ability to create meaningful change.

Second, give consistently. One-time donations are nice, but sustained commitment creates real transformation. The Brown Foundation isn't a project I started and abandoned. It's an ongoing commitment that I've maintained for years and will continue for the rest of my life.

Let me tell you about some of the specific work we're doing right now through the Brown Foundation and The P3 Group, because this is where the rubber meets the road.

We have constructed, financed, and leased healthcare facility projects in Arkansas—critical infrastructure that communities desperately need. These aren't just buildings. They're access points to healthcare for people who've been underserved for generations.

The P3 Group owns student housing at Southeast Arkansas College. This project is meaningful because it allows out-of-state students to attend and live on campus, expanding educational opportunities and bringing diversity to the institution.

We've created endowments and scholarships and made donations to Historically Black Colleges and Universities and Minority-Serving Institutions. We've supported Jackson State University, Alcorn State University, Florida A&M University, University of Arkansas at Pine Bluff, Arkansas State Mid-South, and many others.

Why HBCUs and MSIs? These institutions have been chronically underfunded despite the incredible role they play in educating and developing Black professionals. They've produced generations of leaders, doctors, lawyers, teachers, and entrepreneurs—often with a fraction of the resources that predominantly white institutions receive.

I'm committed to changing that. Through the Brown Foundation, we're providing financial support that helps these institutions continue their vital work.

There are reasons this matters so much to me personally. HBCUs have been the backbone of Black achievement in America. They have educated most Black doctors, lawyers, teachers, and engineers. They've created opportunities when doors were closed everywhere else.

These institutions took students that other schools rejected and turned them into leaders, innovators, and change-makers. They did it with limited resources, with aging facilities, with budgets that were a fraction of what predominantly white institutions received.

And they're still doing it today.

When I support HBCUs through the Brown Foundation, I'm not just writing checks. I'm investing in the future. I'm ensuring that the next generation of Black leaders has the same opportunities that previous generations fought to create.

I'm also recognizing that my success was built on the foundation laid by HBCUs and organizations like the NAACP. They fought the battles that made it possible for me even to enter certain industries. They broke down barriers that would have stopped me from starting.

Now it's my turn to fight those battles for the next generation. It's my turn to break down barriers. It's my turn to create opportunities.

Let me get specific about the scope of our giving back, so you can see that this isn't just talk—it's action.

Through the Brown Foundation, we've made donations and endowments at more than a dozen HBCUs and Minority-Serving Institutions. We're not just supporting one or two schools—we're investing broadly in institutions that serve underrepresented communities across the country.

But our giving goes beyond higher education. We've donated to high schools, helping students who are still finding their path. We've supported food pantries, ensuring that families in our communities don't go hungry. We've contributed to fraternities and sororities that provide mentorship and support networks for young people.

We've sponsored senior trips and field trips for dozens of schools. You might think, "That's nice, but what's the big deal about a field trip?" For many of these students, these trips are their first time leaving their community, their first exposure to museums, universities, or cultural experiences that expand their sense of what's possible. These experiences plant seeds that can grow into dreams.

Here's one example that's meaningful to me: When my former high school football team won its first state championship, I bought championship rings for the entire team and coaching staff. Nobody expected it. But I remembered what it felt like to be a young person with big dreams and limited resources. I remembered the people who believed in me and invested in me when I was coming up.

Those rings weren't just jewelry. They were a message: "Your achievement matters. Your hard work is recognized. Someone who came from where you came from made it, and you can too."

It's what giving back is really about—not just writing checks, but creating moments that inspire, that validate, that show young people their potential.

That's what being self-made really means. It doesn't mean you did it completely alone—nobody does. It means you took the opportunities others created, maximized them, and then created even more opportunities for those coming behind you.

Here's something I want you to understand about commitment: Success in America, particularly for African Americans, requires more than just individual achievement. It requires social contribution. It requires community investment. It requires lifting as you climb.

I've been blessed to work with incredible attorneys, business leaders, and community advocates who understand this principle. We support each other. We create opportunities for each other. We invest in the institutions and initiatives that strengthen our entire community.

That's not just good ethics. That's good business. Because when communities thrive, businesses thrive. When people have opportunities, they create value. When we invest in each other, we all rise together.

The work we're doing through the Brown Foundation—the HBCU endowments, the affordable housing, the food pantry donations, the community development projects—this is all part of a larger vision of creating sustainable prosperity that benefits everyone.

We're also working on affordable housing developments—bringing my work full circle back to where I started, back to the need I saw in my community.

Where I watched family members and friends struggle to find decent and stable housing. Let me be specific about this affordable housing work, because it demonstrates how we're creating sustainable solutions to a problem that affected members of my family.

The Brown Foundation owns and operates two affordable housing communities supported by HUD Housing Assistance Payments contracts, also known as project-based Section 8 assistance. Under a HAP contract, HUD provides monthly rental assistance payments directly to the property owner on behalf of eligible low-income households. It helps ensure the property can be operated sustainably while keeping rents affordable for families who need them most.

These HAP contracts directly benefit low-income families in three critical ways: First, they set rent at an income-based level, so families aren't spending more than they can afford. Second, they provide stable, long-term housing in a specific community, giving families roots and security. Third, they improve housing security by making quality homes attainable even when market rents are completely out of reach.

By owning and operating these HUD-assisted communities, the Brown Foundation is advancing one of its core missions: preserving and providing safe, stable, and affordable housing for families with limited incomes, while maintaining these properties as long-term community assets.

This is personal to me. When I think about family members and friends who struggle to find decent, affordable housing, I'm reminded why this work matters. Every family that finds stable housing through these communities is a family that doesn't have to struggle the way they did. That's not just charity; that's changing the trajectory of families' lives.

We've donated to food pantries, supported community initiatives, and invested in programs that give people the tools and opportunities to improve their lives.

This isn't charity for charity's sake. It is a strategic investment in community development, in education, in creating pathways out of poverty.

Because I know what poverty looks like. I lived it. My mother lived it. And I'm determined to help others escape it the way I did, through education, opportunity, and hard work.

Now, let's discuss how you can do your part.

First, give personally. Don't just write checks and delegate the work. Get involved. Meet the people you're helping. Understand their challenges. Learn from their experiences.

Some of my most valuable insights have come from conversations with young entrepreneurs I'm mentoring and with community members affected by our development projects.

Second, give strategically through your business. The P3 philosophy I discussed earlier is built into the business model, with giving back as a core value. Every project we do creates value for communities, not just for us.

You don't have to separate your business success from your social impact. Integrate them.

Third, give by opening doors. I've used my position on boards and in professional organizations to advocate for other minority entrepreneurs. I've made introductions that have led to opportunities. I've vouched for people who deserved a chance but lacked the connections.

Sometimes the most valuable thing you can give is access.

Giving back has made me more successful, not less. It's expanded my network. It's enhanced my reputation. It's created goodwill that has opened doors I couldn't have opened otherwise.

But more importantly, it's given my success meaning. It's connected my work to a purpose larger than myself. It's ensured that my legacy will be about more than just buildings and bank accounts.

I want to challenge you on something: What are you giving back right now? Not what you plan to give back someday when you're more successful. What are you contributing right now, with the resources and influence you currently have?

You don't have to wait until you're wealthy to make a difference. You can mentor someone today. You can volunteer your expertise today. You can advocate for someone who needs a champion today.

Giving back isn't something you do after you've made it. It's something you do while you're making it.

I also want to address a misconception: Some people think that giving back means sacrificing their own success. That's completely wrong. Giving back enhances your success. It multiplies your impact. It creates a virtuous cycle where everyone rises together.

When I invest in education programs, I'm creating a more skilled workforce that benefits all businesses, including mine. When I support entrepreneurship initiatives, I'm creating more economic activity that strengthens entire communities. When I mentor young leaders, I'm developing the next generation who will carry this work forward.

That's not a sacrifice. That's an investment in a better future for everyone.

Here's another truth about giving back: It's the ultimate test of your character. Anyone can be generous when it's convenient or when there's something to gain. True generosity is giving when it costs you something, when nobody's watching, when there's no immediate return.

I've made commitments to communities and causes that required significant time, money, and energy, with no guarantee of any personal benefit. I did it because it was the right thing to do. I did it because I believe that to whom much is given, much is required.

That's the standard I hold myself to. And it's the standard I challenge you to embrace.

Giving back is contagious. When people see you using your success to lift others, it inspires them to do the same. When you model generosity, you create a culture of generosity.

I've seen this happen in my network. Entrepreneurs I've mentored are now mentoring others. People who've benefited from our community development work are now giving back to their communities. The impact multiplies exponentially.

That's the power of leading by example.

So, here's my challenge: Make giving back a non-negotiable part of your success strategy. Not an afterthought. Not something you'll do someday. A core component of who you are and how you operate.

Identify your cause. Commit to it. Take action. And watch how it transforms not just the lives of those you help, but also your own.

Because here's the ultimate truth: You can't rise to your highest potential while leaving others behind. True success is collective. True wealth is shared. True legacy is measured by the lives you've touched and the opportunities you've created.

Give back—not because you have to, but because it's the path to the most meaningful success you can achieve. In pursuing my impossible dreams, I discovered that the greatest satisfaction comes not from what I've achieved, but from the opportunities I've created for others to pursue their own impossible dreams. That's the true measure of success.

Now let's talk about how to package all this success, impact, and purpose into a brand that represents who you are and what you stand for...

CHAPTER 10 –
BRAND YOURSELF

In the pursuit of the impossible dream, your brand becomes your calling card—the promise that you deliver the extraordinary. This chapter is about building a brand that represents not just who you are but also the impossible dreams you've achieved and what you stand for.

Let me ask you something: When people hear your name, what do they think of? What do they feel? What do they expect?

That's your brand. And whether or not you realize it, you already have one.

The question isn't whether you have a brand. The question is whether you're intentionally building the brand you want or letting others define it for you.

I made a conscious decision years ago to build a brand that represented everything I stood for: Excellence. Self-determination. Success. Style. Substance. That brand is "Self Made."

Self Made isn't just a catchy phrase. It's a philosophy. It's a lifestyle. It's a commitment. And it shows up in everything I do.

Self Made Entertainment. Self Made TV. Self Made with Dee Brown, CEO talk show. Self Made Dee Brown, CEO of luxury custom clothing. Self Made Dee Brown, CEO Sipping Tequila. My yacht was named Self Made.

See the consistency? That's intentional branding.

Building a powerful personal brand must be authentic. You can't fake it. You can't borrow someone else's brand. Build something that genuinely represents who you are and what you stand for.

The Self Made brand works for me because it's my actual story. I didn't inherit wealth. I didn't have connections handed to me. I built everything from the ground up with vision, hard work, and unwavering commitment. Where I'm from, they call that "getting it out the mud." That's what I had to do: "get it out the mud".

That authenticity resonates with people because they can feel it's real.

But authenticity alone isn't enough. You also need consistency. Your brand has to show up the same way across every touchpoint, every interaction, every platform.

When someone sees my clothing line, they should immediately recognize it as part of the same brand as my real estate company, my media ventures, and my other businesses. The quality, the style, the messaging, it all must be consistent.

That consistency builds trust. And trust is the foundation of any strong brand.

Here's how I think about brand building: Your brand is a promise. It's what people can expect when they interact with you, do business with you, or engage with your content.

The Dee Brown brand promises excellence, innovation, and impact. Whether I'm developing a property, producing a television show, or launching a product, people know they'll get something world-class.

That promise must be kept every single time because your brand is only as strong as your most recent interaction.

It's not about being famous. It's about being known for something specific.

I'm not trying to be a celebrity. I'm trying to be recognized as the go-to expert in public-private partnerships, as a successful entrepreneur who's broken barriers, and as someone who's built a diverse empire while giving back to communities.

That specificity makes my brand powerful. When people need expertise in P3s, they think of me. When they want to hear inspiring success stories, they think of me. When they're looking for examples of strategic diversification, they think of me.

That's the power of a well-defined brand. Now, let me give you practical guidance on building your own brand:

First, define your core values. What do you stand for? What's non-negotiable for you? What do you want to be known for?

For me, it's excellence, self-determination, community impact, and continuous growth. Everything I do has to align with those values, or it doesn't get the Dee Brown brand attached to it.

Second, identify your unique positioning. What makes you different? What can you offer that nobody else can?

My unique positioning combines real estate expertise, media savvy, entrepreneurial success, and a commitment to community development. Plenty of people do one or two of those things. Very few do all of them at a high level.

Third, be consistent across all platforms. Your LinkedIn should reflect the same brand as your Instagram, website, business cards, and in-person interactions.

I'm Dee Brown, CEO everywhere. The messaging is consistent. The visual identity is consistent. The quality is consistent.

Fourth, invest in quality. Your brand is reflected in everything you put out into the world. Cheap business cards, poorly designed websites, and low-quality products all damage your brand.

When I launched my luxury clothing line, I didn't cut corners. When I produce television shows, I invest in top-tier production quality. When I publish content, I make sure it's well-written and valuable.

Quality is non-negotiable when you're building a premium brand.

Fifth, tell your story. People connect with narratives, not just credentials. Share your journey. Be vulnerable about your struggles. Celebrate your wins. Let people see the human behind the brand.

That's why I write for Forbes. That's why I host podcasts and television shows. That's why I speak at conferences. I'm constantly telling my story and sharing the lessons I've learned.

That storytelling builds emotional connection, which is the strongest form of branding.

It opens doors. My brand has created opportunities I would never have had access to otherwise.

When Forbes invited me to join their Real Estate Council and Business Council, it was because of the brand I'd built. When I was appointed National Advisor on Public-Private Partnerships, it was because of my brand. When media outlets want expert commentary, they reach out to me because of my brand.

Your brand is your most valuable asset. It's more valuable than any single business, any single property, any single deal.

Because your brand is transferable, it goes with you wherever you go. It opens doors in industries you haven't even entered yet. It creates opportunities you can't even imagine right now.

I also want to talk about brand extensions. Once you've built a strong core brand, you can extend it into new categories.

That's how I went from real estate to media to fashion to spirits to yachting. The Self Made brand was strong enough to carry across all these industries because it represented a lifestyle and a mindset, not just a specific product or service.

But here's the key: Each extension must reinforce the core brand, not dilute it. Every new venture must meet the same standards of excellence. Every new product must deliver on the brand promise.

One subpar product can damage a brand that took years to build.

Consider this about the relationship between personal brand and business success: Your personal brand can become more valuable than any individual business you own.

People do business with people they know, like, and trust. When you have a strong personal brand, you've already established that know-like-trust factor before you even meet someone.

That's why I invest so much in my personal brand through media appearances, speaking engagements, and content creation. It's not ego. It's a strategy.

Here's another aspect of branding that's often overlooked: Your brand should evolve as you evolve. I'm not the same person I was when I started in real estate 32 years ago. My brand has evolved to reflect my growth, my expanded interests, and my deeper understanding of what matters.

But the core values have remained consistent. That's the balance: Evolve without losing your essence.

I also want to address something important: Your brand is built through actions, not just words. You can have the best logo, the slickest website, and the most polished messaging, but if your actions don't align with your brand promise, it all falls apart.

I've built my brand by consistently delivering on my commitments, treating people with respect, operating with integrity, and creating value wherever I go.

It's how you create a brand that lasts.

So, here's my challenge to you: Take control of your brand. Don't let it happen by accident. Don't let others define it for you. Intentionally build a brand that represents the best of who you are and what you stand for.

Define your values. Identify your unique positioning. Be consistent. Invest in quality. Tell your story. And most importantly, back it all up with actions that prove your brand promise is real.

Because in today's world, your brand is your competitive advantage. It's what sets you apart. It's what makes you memorable. It's what creates opportunities. Build it intentionally. Protect it fiercely. Leverage it strategically.

Your brand is your legacy in action. The "Self Made" brand isn't just a name—it's a declaration that impossible dreams are achievable through determination and excellence. Every venture that carries this brand is a testament to pursuing and achieving what others said couldn't be done.

Now let's talk about how to use that brand to lead, influence, and inspire others to reach their own potential...

CHAPTER 11 –
LEADERSHIP AND INFLUENCE

The pursuit of the impossible dream requires leadership, the courage to go first, to show others what's possible, to inspire them to pursue their own impossible dreams. This chapter is about using your success to expand the realm of possibility for others.

Here's a truth that took me years to fully grasp: Success without influence is just personal achievement. But success with influence? That's legacy. I've built businesses. I've accumulated wealth. I've won awards. But none of that matters as much as the lives I've influenced, the leaders I've developed, and the movements I've contributed to.

That's what real leadership is about: Using your platform, your resources, and your experience to elevate others.

I serve on the Documentary and Nonfiction Committee for the Producers Guild of America. I've served on the board of directors for the U.S. Minority Contractors' Association across multiple regions. I was appointed National

Advisor on Public-Private Partnerships and Urban Redevelopment for the 79th President of the National Bar Association.

These aren't just titles to add to my resume. They're platforms for influence. They're opportunities to shape industries, advocate for change, and create pathways for others.

That's how I think about leadership: It's stewardship of influence. This is what I've learned about leadership over three decades of building businesses and organizations:

First, leadership is about vision. Anyone can manage what exists. Leaders create what doesn't exist yet. They see possibilities that others miss. They articulate a future that inspires people to action.

When I founded The P3 Group, I wasn't just starting another construction company. I was casting a vision for how the public and private sectors could work together to transform communities. That vision attracted talented people, committed partners, and significant resources.

Vision is magnetic. It pulls people toward a future they want to be part of.

Second, leadership is about service. The best leaders I know don't lead from a position of superiority. They lead from a position of service. They ask, "How can I help my team succeed? How can I remove obstacles? How can I create conditions for excellence?"

That's how I approach leadership in all my ventures. I'm not there to be served. I'm there to serve the mission, serve the team, and serve the communities we impact. When you lead through service, people don't follow you because they must. They follow you because they want to.

Third, leadership is about development. Your job as a leader isn't to be the smartest person in the room. It's to make everyone in the room smarter.

I invest heavily in developing the people around me. I mentor young entrepreneurs. I create opportunities for team members to stretch and grow. I share knowledge freely because I know that my success is multiplied when I develop others' success.

The best leaders are talent developers, not talent hoarders.

Fourth, leadership is about integrity. Your influence is only as strong as your character. If people can't trust you, they won't follow you—at least not for long. I've built my reputation for keeping my word, operating with transparency, and doing what's right, even when it's not easy. That integrity has become an invaluable asset.

In a world where trust is scarce, integrity is your competitive advantage.

Fifth, leadership is about courage. Leading means deciding when you don't have all the information. It means taking unpopular stands. It means being the first to try something new.

Owning the golf course required courage. When I pioneered public-private partnerships in spaces where minorities weren't present, that required courage. When I expanded into media, fashion, and spirits, that required courage.

Leadership and comfort don't coexist. If you're always comfortable, you're probably not leading.

Now, let me talk specifically about influence. Influence differs from authority. Authority is positional; it comes with a title or role. Influence is relational; it's earned through credibility, consistency, and contribution.

I have influence in the real estate development industry, not because of my title, but because of my track record. I have influence in the media, not because I demand it, but because I've created content that adds value. I have influence in entrepreneurship circles not because I'm the loudest voice, but because I've walked the walk.

That's how you build real influence: Through demonstrated excellence over time.

Influence is a responsibility, not just a privilege. When people listen to what you say, model their behavior after yours, and decide based on your guidance, that's a sacred trust.

I take that responsibility seriously. That's why I'm careful about what I say publicly. That's why I'm intentional about the example I set. That's why I invest time in mentoring and teaching, even when there's no immediate benefit to me.

Because influence without responsibility is dangerous.

Here are some practical ways I've leveraged my influence:

Through media: My podcast "The Sky's the Limit: Beyond the Deal" reaches an international audience. My television shows "Self Made" and "#HBCYou" reach communities across the country. My articles in Forbes and Entrepreneur reach millions of readers. Each of these platforms is an opportunity to influence thinking, inspire action, and share knowledge.

Through speaking: I speak at conferences, universities, and organizations about entrepreneurship, P3s, and breaking barriers. Every speaking engagement is a chance to plant seeds that might grow into someone else's success story.

Through mentorship, I mentor young entrepreneurs, sharing not just what worked for me but also what didn't. The failures are often more valuable lessons than the successes.

Through advocacy, I use my board and professional organization positions to advance policies and practices that create opportunities for minorities and underserved communities.

Through example: Perhaps most importantly, I lead by example. I show what's possible. I demonstrate barriers can be broken. I prove you can build wealth while building communities.

That's influence in action.

You need to understand this about maximizing your influence:

First, be generous with your knowledge. Some people hoard information because they think it gives them power. But influence actually grows when you share what you know. The more you give, the more your influence expands.

Second, be consistent. Influence is built through repeated demonstrations of your values and capabilities. One great speech doesn't create influence. One successful project doesn't create influence. Consistent excellence over time creates influence.

Third, be authentic. People can sense when you're being fake. They can tell when you're performing versus when you're being real. Authentic influence is more powerful and more sustainable than a manufactured image.

Fourth, be strategic. Not every opportunity to influence is worth taking. Focus your influence where you can make the most impact, where it aligns with your values, and where it serves your larger mission.

Fifth, be humble. The moment you believe your own hype, your influence declines. Stay grounded. Stay teachable. Stay connected to the people and communities you're trying to serve.

I've received recognition from many organizations and agencies, but I don't let those accolades go to my head. They're not about me. They're about the work, the impact, and the example.

Let me also talk about the relationship between leadership and followership. Great leaders are also great followers. They know when to lead and when to support someone else's leadership.

As a member of Kappa Alpha Psi Fraternity, and many other organizations, I'm not always the leader. Sometimes I'm a supporter, a contributor, or a team member.

That willingness to follow makes me a better leader. It keeps me humble. It reminds me that leadership is about the mission, not about my ego.

Leadership can be lonely sometimes. You'll make decisions that others don't understand. You'll see things others don't. You'll carry burdens that others don't know about.

That's part of the responsibility. But it's also why building a strong support system is so important. You need people who can speak truth to you, challenge your thinking, and support you when the weight feels too heavy.

Leadership isn't a solo journey. It's a team sport.

So, here's my challenge to you: Step into your leadership. Stop waiting for someone to give you permission. Stop waiting until you feel ready. Stop waiting until you have all the answers.

Lead from where you are, with what you have, for the people who need what you can offer.

Your influence is needed. Your leadership is required. Your voice matters.

Use it wisely. Use it generously. Use it courageously.

Because the world doesn't need more followers, it needs more leaders who will serve, sacrifice, and show the way. Leadership in the pursuit of the impossible dream means showing others that barriers can be broken, that limitations are lies, and that their own impossible dreams are within reach. Every person I mentor, every barrier I break, every example I set—it all expands what others believe is possible.

Now let's talk about what happens when you combine everything we've discussed—the dreams, the education, the resilience, the diversification, the giving back, the branding, and the leadership...

CHAPTER 12 –
THE SKY'S THE LIMIT

The pursuit of the impossible dream never ends. This chapter is about understanding that there are no limits except the ones you accept, that every impossible dream achieved reveals the next impossible dream to pursue.

You know what I love about the phrase "the sky's the limit"? It's not actually true because even the sky isn't the limit anymore.

We've been to the moon. We've sent probes beyond our solar system. We're planning missions to Mars. The sky isn't the limit; it's just the beginning. "The Sky's the Limit" isn't just a phrase; it's a philosophy for pursuing the impossible dream. It means that achieving one impossible dream doesn't mean you're done. It means you're ready for the next one. My journey from real estate to media to fashion to spirits was an impossible dream that led to the next.

And that's exactly how I want you to think about your potential: There are no limits except the ones you accept. When I named my podcast "The Sky's the Limit: Beyond the Deal," I was making a statement about possibility. I was declaring that we're not bound by conventional thinking, traditional limitations, or other people's expectations.

We're only bound by our imagination and our willingness to act on it.

This is what "beyond the deal" means to me: thinking bigger than the transaction at hand. It means seeing opportunities where others see obstacles. It means building legacies, not just businesses. It means creating an impact that extends far beyond your immediate circle.

That mindset has allowed me to build The P3 Group into the nation's leading African American-owned public-private partnership real estate development firm. That mindset has enabled me to expand into media, fashion, spirits, and yachting. That mindset has driven me to win awards.

Understand, I'm not special. I'm not more talented than you. I'm not smarter than you. I don't have access to resources that you can't access.

What I have is a refusal to accept limitations. What I have is a commitment to continuous growth. What I believe is that the best is always yet to come.

And you can have that too.

This is what continuous growth looks like in practice: It means never being satisfied with where you are. Not in a negative, never-enough way. But in a positive, always-expanding way.

I'm proud of what I've built. But I'm more excited about what I'm building next. I celebrate my achievements. But I'm more focused on my next goals. That forward momentum is what keeps life exciting. It's what keeps you relevant. It's what keeps you growing.

This is what I've learned: The moment you think you've arrived is the moment you start declining. There is no arrival. There's only a continuous journey.

I could have stopped after building a successful construction company. I could have stopped after establishing The P3 Group. I could have stopped after becoming the first African American to own a golf course in Arkansas.

But why would I stop? Why would I limit myself to what I've already accomplished when there's so much more I can create, so much more I can contribute, so much more I can become?

But let me pause here and address something important, a question I ask myself regularly: When is enough, enough?

I treat that question as a checkpoint, not a signal to stop. It's a moment to make sure I'm still building for the right reasons. "I'm not done" isn't about chasing numbers or seeking validation. It's about purpose.

As I grow through real estate, partnerships, construction, media, and philanthropy, each new level increases my ability to create opportunities and leave a lasting impact. It drives me forward, not accumulation, but the expanding capacity to make a difference.

I've learned to balance ambition with contentment by separating "enough" from "more." Enough means peace, health, family, and gratitude, the things that truly matter. More means greater impact, wider reach, and deeper contribution. I reassess constantly to make sure that pursuing "more" never threatens what's already "enough."

I define success as alignment, not accumulation. And I build in intentional pauses to reflect and celebrate progress, to make sure I'm not just moving fast but moving in the right direction.

Ultimately, "enough is enough" when the pursuit stops serving the mission. But if the work stays aligned with my values and meaningful to the communities I serve, I'm still moving forward. The sky's the limit means you never stop reaching.

Let me talk about what's next for me, because I want you to see that this mindset never stops:

I'm expanding The P3 Group into new markets. I'm developing new media properties. I'm growing my fashion and spirits brands. I'm exploring opportunities in technology and innovation. I'm deepening my philanthropic work through the Brown Foundation.

Let me be specific about what's coming next, because this is where vision meets action:

We're working on additional healthcare facilities in Arkansas and beyond—critical infrastructure that will serve communities for decades. We're expanding our student housing developments to more colleges and universities, creating opportunities for students who otherwise couldn't afford to attend.

We're developing more affordable housing projects, bringing quality living spaces to families who need them most. This work is meaningful to me because it connects directly to my mother's struggle and my earliest inspiration.

Through the Brown Foundation, we're increasing our support for HBCU endowments. We're not just making one-time donations—we're creating sustainable funding streams that will support these institutions for years to come.

We're also exploring new ways to leverage private-sector resources to fund public-sector needs. That's the P3 model in action—finding creative ways to bring together different resources to solve community problems.

Every project we complete opens the door to the next one. Every success creates credibility for bigger opportunities. Every barrier we break makes it easier for others to follow.

This isn't just about building my empire. It's about creating a model that others can replicate, proving you can do well financially while doing good for society, and demonstrating that business can be a force for positive change.

And I'm doing all of this while maintaining excellence in everything I'm already doing.

That's not spreading myself too thin. That's living fully. That's maximizing my potential. That's refusing to accept artificial limits.

Now, let me give you some practical guidance on how to adopt this "sky's the limit" mindset: First, regularly expand your vision. What seemed impossible five years ago might now be routine. What seems impossible today might be your reality five years from now.

I regularly sit down and ask myself: "What would I attempt if I knew I couldn't fail?" Then I work backward from that vision to create a plan.

Second, surround yourself with people who think bigger than you do. If you're the most ambitious person in your circle, you need a new circle.

Become part of organizations where the baseline is excellence, and the expectation is continuous growth.

Third, invest in continuous learning. The world is changing faster than ever. The skills that got you here won't necessarily get you there. Stay curious. Stay hungry. Stay learning. I'm constantly reading, attending conferences, taking courses, and seeking new knowledge. That investment in learning keeps me competitive and relevant.

Fourth, take calculated risks. Playing it safe might protect what you have, but it won't get you where you want to go. Be willing to risk failure in pursuit of greater success.

Every major breakthrough in my career came from taking a risk that others thought was too big, too bold, or too ambitious. Fifth, celebrate progress as you pursue more. Don't wait until you've "made it" to enjoy your life. Celebrate the wins along the way. Enjoy the journey. But keep moving forward.

Here's something else about the "sky's the limit" mindset: It's contagious. When people see you continuously growing, achieving, and breaking through barriers, it gives them permission to do the same. That's why I'm so public about my journey. That's why I write articles, host shows, speak at events, and now write this book. I want people to see what's possible. I want them to raise their own expectations. I want them to refuse to accept limitations.

Your growth inspires others to grow. Your success creates permission for others to succeed. Your refusal to accept limits expands the realm of possibility for everyone watching.

Let me also talk about what happens when you combine all the principles we've discussed in this book:

When you understand your foundation and honor those who sacrificed for you (Chapter 1), you gain the purpose and motivation to dream big (Chapter 2) and build a strong educational foundation (Chapter 3), creating the capability to achieve extraordinary things.

When you break barriers (Chapter 4), you create opportunities that didn't exist before.

When you face your greatest fall and rise again (Chapter 5), you discover setbacks are setups for comebacks—and that your lowest point can become the foundation for your greatest achievements.

When you apply the P3 philosophy (Chapter 6) and develop resilience through adversity (Chapter 7), you build sustainable success that can weather any storm.

When you diversify your vision (Chapter 8), give back (Chapter 9), and build a strong brand (Chapter 10), you create an impact that extends far beyond your immediate success.

When you lead with influence (Chapter 11) and maintain a "sky's the limit" mindset (Chapter 12), you become unstoppable.

That's the compound effect of these principles working together. Each one reinforces the others. Each one multiplies the impact of the others.

And the result? A life of extraordinary achievement, meaningful impact, and continuous growth.

Understand you're capable of so much more than you currently believe. The limitations you've accepted aren't real. The barriers you see aren't permanent. The ceiling you've bumped up against isn't the top.

There's always another level. There's always more growth available. There's always a greater impact possible.

The question is: Are you willing to reach for it? I've received many accolades and awards.

But you know what? I'm not done. Not even close.

Because the sky's the limit means there's always more to achieve, more to contribute, more to become. And the same is true for you.

So, here's my challenge: Stop accepting limitations. Stop playing small and stop waiting for permission.

Start dreaming bigger and start acting bolder. Start believing that the best version of your life is still ahead of you.

Because it is, the sky isn't the limit. It's just the beginning.

Now let's bring everything together and create your personal blueprint for success...

CHAPTER 13 – YOUR BLUEPRINT FOR SUCCESS

This blueprint is your roadmap to pursuing the impossible dream. Every principle, every strategy, every lesson in this chapter helps you achieve what others say can't be done.

We've covered a lot of ground together in this book. We've talked about dreaming big, building foundations, breaking barriers, creating partnerships, developing resilience, diversifying your vision, giving back, building your brand, leading with influence, and refusing to accept limits.

Now it's time to bring it all together into a practical blueprint that you can use to build your own extraordinary success.

This isn't theory. It isn't motivational fluff. It is a proven system I've used to build multiple successful businesses, overcome barriers, and create lasting impact.

And it will work for you too—if you're willing to do the work.

Let me give you the step-by-step blueprint:

STEP 1: DEFINE YOUR VISION

Get crystal clear on what you want to achieve. Not what others expect of you. Not what seems realistic. What do YOU truly want?

Write it down in vivid detail. What does success look like to you? What impact do you want to make? What legacy do you want to leave?

This vision becomes your North Star. Every decision, every action, every investment should move you closer to this vision.

STEP 2: BUILD YOUR FOUNDATION

Invest in education—formal and informal. Develop the skills, knowledge, and expertise you need to compete at the highest level.

This isn't optional. It is the foundation on which everything else is built. The stronger your foundation, the higher you can build.

Commit to being a lifelong learner. Read voraciously. Take courses. Seek mentors. Attend conferences. Never stop developing yourself.

STEP 3: IDENTIFY YOUR BARRIERS

What's standing between you and your vision? Be honest. Be specific.

Is it a lack of capital? Lack of connections? Lack of knowledge? Systemic barriers? Personal limitations?

You can't break through barriers you haven't identified. Name them. Study them. Understand them.

STEP 4: DEVELOP YOUR STRATEGY

How will you overcome those barriers? What resources do you need? What partnerships could help? What skills do you need to develop?

Create a detailed plan. Not just what you'll do, but when you'll do it, how you'll measure progress, and what success looks like at each stage.

Strategy without execution is just dreaming. But execution without strategy is just activity. You need both.

STEP 5: BUILD YOUR TEAM

You cannot do this alone. Identify the people you need around you: mentors, partners, team members, advisors, and supporters.

Invest in relationships. Be generous with others. Create value for your network. Build a reputation for delivering on commitments.

The quality of your team will determine the quality of your outcomes.

STEP 6: TAKE MASSIVE ACTION

Stop planning and start doing. Take the first step, even if you don't have everything figured out. Take the next step. And the next one.

Momentum is built through action, not through thinking about action.

I didn't wait until I had every detail of public-private partnerships figured out before starting The P3 Group. I learned by doing. You will too.

STEP 7: PROTECT YOURSELF AND DOCUMENT EVERYTHING

As you build success, protect yourself legally and professionally. Document important conversations and agreements. Get independent legal advice on complex transactions. Keep detailed records.

I learned this lesson the hard way during my indictment. That recording I made of the lender's confession became crucial evidence. The documentation I maintained helped prove my case. The independent legal opinions I'd obtained showed I'd done my due diligence.

Don't assume that doing the right thing is enough protection. In business, especially when you're breaking barriers and achieving at high levels, you need to protect yourself with documentation, legal counsel, and careful record-keeping.

This isn't paranoia—it's wisdom.

STEP 8: PREPARE FOR ADVERSITY AND BUILD RESILIENCE

You will face setbacks. You will encounter obstacles. You will experience failures. And if you're successful enough, you may even face injustice.

That's not a possibility—it's a guarantee.

Build your resilience in advance through physical, mental, and spiritual practices, as well as strong relationships. When adversity hits—whether it's a failed deal or an 81-count federal indictment—you'll have reserves to draw from.

I rebuilt my entire career after losing everything at age 31. Every achievement I've had since then—the golf course, the Navy contract, building the nation's leading minority-owned P3 firm, the 150+ awards—all of it came AFTER my greatest fall.

Remember: Your lowest point can become the foundation for your greatest achievements. Setbacks are setups for comebacks. The question isn't whether you'll face adversity—it's how you'll respond when you do.

STEP 9: DIVERSIFY STRATEGICALLY

Once you've established success in one area, look for adjacent opportunities. How can you leverage your existing strengths, relationships, and reputation into new ventures?

But remember: Diversify from strength, not weakness. And make sure each new venture reinforces your core brand.

STEP 10: GIVE BACK CONSISTENTLY

Build giving back into your success from the beginning. Don't wait until you've "made it."

Identify causes that align with your values. Make consistent commitments. Get involved.

Your success will be more meaningful, more sustainable, and more impactful when it's connected to a purpose larger than yourself.

STEP 11: BUILD YOUR BRAND

Be intentional about how you're perceived. What do you want to be known for? What promise are you making to the world?

Be consistent across all platforms. Invest in quality. Tell your story. Back up your brand with actions that prove it's real.

Your brand is your most valuable asset. Protect it. Nurture it. Leverage it.

STEP 12: LEAD AND INFLUENCE

Use your success to create opportunities for others. Mentor. Advocate. Teach. Share.

Your influence is a responsibility, not just a privilege. Use it to expand the possibilities for others.

The true measure of your success is the success you enable in others.

STEP 13: NEVER STOP GROWING

The moment you think you've arrived is the moment you start declining. There is no finish line. There's only continuous growth.

Keep dreaming bigger. Keep learning more. Keep achieving more and keep contributing more.

The sky's the limit and beyond.

Now, let me give you some final thoughts as we close this journey together:

Success is not a destination. It's a direction. It's not something you achieve once and then maintain. It's something you pursue continuously with passion, purpose, and persistence.

I've built The P3 Group into the nation's leading African American-owned public-private partnership real estate development firm. I've become the first African American owner of an 18-hole golf course in Arkansas and the Mid-South region. I've won awards. I've built a media empire, a fashion line, a spirits brand, and much more.

But I'm not telling you this to impress you. I'm telling you this to show you what's possible.

If a kid with a dream and a commitment to excellence can build all of this, imagine what you can build with the same commitment. You have everything you need to succeed. You have the intelligence. You have the capability. You have the potential.

What you might not have yet is the belief. The belief that you can do it. The belief that you deserve it. The belief that it's possible for someone like you.

That's what I hope this book has given you: Belief.

Belief that barriers can be broken. Belief that dreams can become reality. Belief that you can build something extraordinary while making a meaningful difference in the world.

I believe in you. Now you need to believe in yourself.

Take this blueprint. Apply it to your life. Adapt it to your circumstances. Make it your own and then build something amazing.

Build businesses that create value. Build wealth that creates opportunities. Build a brand that inspires others. Build a legacy that outlasts you.

The world needs what you have to offer.

Don't play small. Don't hold back. Don't wait for permission.

Start today. Start now. Start where you are with what you have.

And remember: The sky isn't the limit. It's just the beginning.

I've shared my story with you. I've given you the principles that have guided my success. I've provided you with a blueprint to follow.

Now it's your turn, your turn to dream. Your turn to build. Your turn to break barriers. Your turn to create an impact. Your turn to leave a legacy. I can't wait to see what you build. I can't wait to hear your success story.

I can't wait to see how you use these principles to create your own extraordinary life.

Because here's what I know for certain: If I can do it, you can do it.

If I can overcome obstacles, you can too.

If I can break through barriers, you can too.

If I can build an empire while giving back to communities, you can too.

The only question is: Will you?

Will you commit to the journey? Will you do the work? Will you refuse to accept limitations? Will you keep going when it gets hard? Will you believe in yourself even when others doubt you?

I hope the answer is yes.

Because the world needs more people who will dream big, work hard, give back, and inspire others.

The world needs more people who refuse to accept the status quo and instead create the future they want to see.

The world needs more people who are truly self-made. So, make it happen.

Build your empire. Break your barriers. Create your legacy. And when you do, reach back and help someone else do the same. That's how we all rise together. That's how we create a world where everyone can reach their full potential.

That's how we prove that the sky truly isn't the limit; it's just the beginning.

Now go. Your extraordinary life is waiting for you!

www.ingramcontent.com/pod-product-compliance
Lightning Source LLC
Chambersburg PA
CBHW050006040726
47599CB00014B/1238